Global Markets and Government Regulation in Telecommunications

In recent years, liberalization, privatization, and deregulation have become commonplace in sectors once dominated by government-owned monopolies. In telecommunications, for example, during the 1990s, more than 129 countries established independent regulatory agencies and more than 100 countries privatized the state-owned telecom operator. Why did so many countries liberalize in such a short period of time? For example, why did both Denmark and Burundi, nations different along so many relevant dimensions, liberalize their telecom sectors around the same time?

Kirsten Rodine-Hardy argues that international organizations – not national governments or market forces – are the primary drivers of policy convergence in the important arena of telecommunications regulation: they create and shape preferences for reform and provide forums for expert discussions and the emergence of policy standards. Yet she also shows that international convergence leaves room for substantial variation among countries, using both econometric analysis and controlled case comparisons of eight European countries.

Kirsten Rodine-Hardy is an assistant professor of political science at Northeastern University, where she teaches international political economy, comparative politics, and European politics. She completed her Ph.D. in political science at the University of California, Berkeley, and spent two years at Harvard University on a pre-dissertation fellowship. She earned degrees from Brown University (AB honors and magna cum laude) and Georgetown University (MSFS in international trade and finance), and she studied at the Institut d'Etudes Politiques in Paris and at the ICPSR at Michigan University. She was a visiting assistant professor at Brown University in 2005 and 2006. She has received research support from the University of California's Institute for Cooperation and Conflict and the Berkeley Post-Soviet Studies Program, and she has consulted for the World Bank, the Organization for Economic Cooperation and Development, and the European Union. She participates actively in the American Political Science Association, Midwest Political Science Association, and International Studies Association. She is affiliated with Harvard University's Minda de Gunzburg Center for European Studies and the Northeastern University Center for Emerging Markets, based at the Northeastern School of Business.

Global Markets and Government Regulation in Telecommunications

KIRSTEN RODINE-HARDY
Northeastern University

CAMBRIDGE
UNIVERSITY PRESS

CAMBRIDGE UNIVERSITY PRESS
Cambridge, New York, Melbourne, Madrid, Cape Town,
Singapore, São Paulo, Delhi, Mexico City

Cambridge University Press
32 Avenue of the Americas, New York, NY 10013-2473, USA

www.cambridge.org
Information on this title: www.cambridge.org/9781107022607

First published 2013

Printed in the United States of America

A catalog record for this publication is available from the British Library.

Library of Congress Cataloging in Publication Data
Rodine-Hardy, Kirsten.
Global markets and government regulation in telecommunications / Kirsten
Rodine-Hardy, Northeastern University.
pages cm
Includes bibliographical references.
ISBN 978-1-107-02260-7
1. Telecommunication policy. 2. Deregulation. I. Title.
HE7645.R635 2013
384–dc23 2012031867

ISBN 978-1-107-02260-7 Hardback

In loving memory of

Paul Jay Hardy, Jr., 1961–2011

Contents

List of Figures and Tables

FIGURES

TABLES

Acknowledgments

The globalization of telecommunications has taken place during my lifetime, and I remember having to wait in line at the post office in France to call my parents in the United States. I also remember the excitement of the Minitel in France in the mid-1980s, and the promise of phone cards that would make calling from a phone booth both easier and cheaper. Later, back in the United States, I took a class at Georgetown University on international telecommunications with Wilson Dizard and took a tour of Intelsat's headquarters, where I learned about international telecommunications. One of the big questions in the late 1980s was how to analyze recent market developments in Argentina and Mexico, particularly as possible examples for a new wave of Eastern European countries that entered the global markets in 1989, at the end of the Cold War. I wrote a research paper on the Hungarian telecommunications system, such as it was at the time, and I was able to do more research while in an internship on telecommunications at the Center for Strategic and International Studies (CSIS) in Washington, D.C. That year, I had the opportunity to move to Prague, where it was easier to call my parents from a phone booth in the middle of a field using an AT&T calling card than to call my friends around the corner, who were lucky enough to have a barely functional phone on their dorm room floor. After four years of working in private sector development in Central Europe while living in Prague, I spent some time working in Washington, D.C., did some short-term work with the World Bank and a few telecommunications-related organizations, and then returned to graduate school to pursue more studies in international political economy at the University of California, Berkeley.

Observing the processes of globalization, liberal market reforms, and democratization firsthand in Central Europe, I deepened my interest in the political economy of markets and government regulations. I chose telecommunications as a lens through which to analyze governments as they interact with global markets, especially in the context of globalization, Europeanization, and liberal reforms. I observed the movement of international organizations and elites, and how bureaucrats in the former state-owned telecommunications firms transformed into new regulators for a dynamic and unfolding market, with implications for prices and availability of services for consumers, and prospects for connecting with the broader world. These new regulatory agencies, similar in form, became responsible for setting the terms for powerful international firms and ensuring the availability of products and services for a wide population. It is now possible to communicate simultaneously with friends in multiple countries, all using technology I can hold in my hand. How global markets and government regulation affect the opportunities and resources for information access and prosperity remain enduring questions for me, and form the basis for this book.

This book began to take shape as a dissertation at UC Berkeley, and I first thank my committee for their unfailing support and constructive criticism: co-chairs Beth Simmons and Steve Vogel, Henry Brady, and Howard Shelanski. I received support from the Institute on Global Conflict and Cooperation (IGCC) and the Berkeley Post-Soviet Studies Program. I also received a dissertation fellowship from Harvard University, where I spent two years finishing research and writing. I received support from the Weatherhead Center for International Affairs, and later joined Harvard's Minda da Gunzburg Center for European Studies.

I transformed the book project during my time at Northeastern University, and I thank my wonderful colleagues there: Amílcar Barreto, Chris Bosso, Denise Garcia, Ronald Hedlund, Denise Horn, David Lazer, Suzanne Ogden, John Portz, and Michael

Tolley have provided much-needed mentorship, guidance, and encouragement. I could not ask for a more collegial environment, and I thank my entire department, as well as my students, who keep me engaged, inspired, and informed. Ian McManus, Krista Denofrio, and Beth Boorman provided amazing research assistance. I also thank the editor, Lew Bateman, and the editorial staff at Cambridge and two anonymous reviewers who made invaluable comments that strengthened the manuscript considerably. All mistakes remain my own.

I also extend thanks to all those telecom specialists, regulators, and practitioners in the Czech Republic, Slovakia, Hungary, the Netherlands, Washington, D.C., and Geneva, Switzerland, who graciously provided their time and valuable expertise during my research visits. A limited list includes Doreen Bogdan-Martin, Nancy Sundberg, Tim Kelly, Esperanza Magpantay (ITU), Diane Steinour (Department of Commerce), Irene Wu, John Giusti (FCC), and Dmitri Ypsilanti (OECD). Others agreed to be interviewed only under the condition that they not be named, and I thank them profusely.

Other academics have provided most helpful comments and critiques during conferences and meetings, including Moises Arce, Andy Baker, Sarah Brooks, David Coen, Derrick Cogburn, Barbara Connolly, Peter Cowhey, Michelle Dion, Henry Farrell, Nanette Levinson, Abe Newman, Craig Parsons, J. P. Singh, and A. Maria Toyoda.

I would like to extend special thanks to Anne Clunan and Rosie Hsueh, whose wholehearted support has helped me so much. Data gurus include Nancy Brune, Zachary Elkins, John Gerring, Tracy Gordon, Alexandra Guisinger, Sonal Pandya, and John Sides.

The following friends have provided moral support and guidance, especially the Lerret family – Anker, Dibba, Elizabeth, Mark, and Matthew. I also thank Brad Abrams, Alison Adams, Melanie Adem, Angela and Michael Allen, Elif Armbruster, Caroline Arnold, Christopher Beecroft, Pamela Beecroft, Robert and Mette Beecroft, Karlo Berger, Ruth Berry, Heather Blair, Leslie Bliss, Krista and Larry Bradley, Amey Callahan, Melani

Cammett, Laura Caputo, Meg Carne, Annabel Cellini, Rachael Cobb, Kathleen Coleman, Sarah Corvene, Tanya Cosway, Mary Dineen, Kate Doherty, Jules Elkins, Merve Emre, Christine Erbacher, Sarah Flack, Carolyn Foug, Vanna Gonzales and Curtis Barnes, Linda Goorin, Jan Gough, Vera Grant, Faxon Green, Jill Greenlee, Bethany Grella, Ida Grum, Matt Haber, Jo-Anne Hart, Alexandra Hawley, Rosie Hsueh, Heather Hurlburt, Dana Hyde, Michel Ishakian, Julie Kahn, Peggy Karns, Nina Katchadourian, Ingrid Kleespies, Lauren Kopans, Irene Krarup, Dan Kronenfeld, Jennifer Dossa Lamonte, Loren Landau, Michael Langlois, Ellen Lawton, Janet Livingstone, Darren and Gwen MacCaughey, Christina and Haldan Martinson, Karen Mathiasen, Tim Matthews, Angela McIntyre, Maria Miller, Rachel Mitchell, Sarah and Matt Mowbray, Megan Mullin, Michael Murray, Fiona Nauseda, Conor O'Dwyer, Rebecca Olson, Nathan Paxton, Kathryn Pearson, Barbie Pizzotti, Eliot Posner, Diahanna Post, Beth and Adam Pulzetti, Jennie Rathbun, Pearl Riney, Susan Root, Sara Sclaroff, David Singer, Anne Stauffer, Danielle Horton Taylor, Amy Timmins, Rachel Tritt, David and Isabel Tumblin, Mark Vail, Lisa Walker, Kelly Whitney, Serene Wille, John Waugh Wright, Debbie Yalen, Rachel Zauderer, Daniel Ziblatt, and the choirs at St. Mark's Berkeley and Christ Church Cambridge. I also thank the canines: Chili, Molly, and Monty, and in memory of Jet and Chester.

I thank my many communities of support, especially those members of the Circle H Ranch Hands, who provided meals, rides, humor, love, and support during some dark times. I am grateful for the ministers of Christ Church Cambridge, Mark Bozzuti-Jones, Joe Robinson, Jeff Mello, Jonathan Eden, and Stuart Forster, and the kindness and hospitality of the Sisters and associates at the Bethany House of Prayer, especially Mary Meader and Julia Slayton. I also thank those members of my other spiritual communities who prefer not to be named, for giving me the strength to live life on life's terms.

I also thank my family, especially my incredible brother and sister-in-law, Paul and Jennifer Rodine, and my nieces Amalia and Theodora. In loving memory of my father, Dr. Elward T. Rodine, and my grandparents, Dr. Milward T. Rodine, Elsie Rodine, the Reverend Bernard Spong, and Dr. Doris Spong. I also thank Louise Rodine Doucette, Edward Doucette, Soterios and Elizabeth Stavrou, and the rest of the Ahlbergs, Rodines, Spongs, Stavrous, and Walthers.

Finally, in memory of my beloved husband, Paul Jay Hardy, Jr. (1961–2011), for his kindness, abiding love, strength, and humor. I will keep him forever in my heart. And to our children, Eleanor and David – thank you for keeping me focused on the most important things in life – love, family, connection, humor, and music.

Preface

> Ninety percent of the world market has embraced the paradigm shift of competition, privatization, and liberalization.
>
> –Yoshio Utsumi, Secretary General of the International Telecommunications Union, *Financial Times* October 13, 2003

Forces of globalization have transformed the political and economic landscape in countries around the world, in areas ranging from economic policy to social policy. In recent years, liberalization, privatization, and deregulation have become commonplace in sectors once dominated by government-owned monopolies. Some of these shifts came with stunning speed, and on an unexpectedly global level. In telecommunications, for example, during the 1990s, more than 158 countries established new independent regulatory agencies and more than 126 countries privatized the state-owned telecom incumbent operator. Why did so many countries liberalize in such a short period of time? For example, why did both Denmark and Burundi, nations different along so many relevant dimensions, liberalize their telecom sectors around the same time?

I demonstrate how global markets affect domestic institutional innovations through a key mechanism of diffusion – through the interaction of international organizations and domestic states' governments. I argue that international organizations – and not national governments or global market forces – are the primary drivers of policy convergence in the important arena of telecommunications regulation. I show that international organizations play a critical role in the diffusion of domestic institutional innovations in three ways: they help create and shape preferences for reform, they provide forums for expert discussions, and they provide forums for the emergence of policy standards within the emerging regime for telecommunications regulation. Yet, I also show that international organizations and international policy convergence leave room for substantial variation among the national cases. I also carefully assess the balance between the international pressures that produce convergence and the domestic factors that account for national variations.

THE DIFFUSION OF INNOVATION THROUGH MEMBERSHIP IN INTERNATIONAL INSTITUTIONS

This book addresses this important gap in the diffusion literature, as well as in conventional political economy explanations, by identifying specific actors and mechanisms associated with policy innovation in the telecommunications sector. In this regard, the diffusion of regulatory reform is said to occur when the prior adoption of a practice by one or more countries, such as the establishment of a separate regulatory authority, affects the probability of adoption in those countries that retain monopolistic, closed, telecommunications markets. The mechanisms for diffusion are critical, and this book argues that they reside in no small part in nations' participation in international organizations. This argument builds upon some recent work in socialization theory and developments in international law (Johnston 2008; Raustiala 2002; Slaughter 2004).

Socialization through international organizations (in the three ways noted) helps explain many aspects of liberal policy adoption, from the overall direction of reform to the timing of reform enactment and some of the specific substantive regulations enacted. I argue that economic policy choice is conditioned by the choices of other countries and international organizations, but that countries do not merely receive policies "from above," either through mechanisms of coercion or purely through top-down teaching. Yet, socialization through international organizations may not affect all aspects of market-oriented telecommunications reform. Some of the scope conditions for this kind of argument may only apply in conditions of high uncertainty, with a substantial ideological consensus in favor of the appropriateness of the proposed policy innovations (e.g., the establishment of a new, separate telecom agency). For example, it may be that market competition best explains the spread of liberalization, and that domestic political and economic configurations coupled with a lack of global ideological consensus on privatization best explain the privatization (or lack thereof) of the state-owned telecom operator.

I first argue that international policy diffusion plays a critical role in explaining the spread and shape of liberal telecom reforms. Next, I show that international organizations are key actors and agents of diffusion in developing and promoting policies for regulatory reform in telecommunications. International organizations help create and shape preferences for reform and also provide forums for expert discussions and the emergence of policy standards within the new regime for telecom regulation.

Yet, although diffusion is one understudied factor critical to understanding the spread of liberal reforms in key policy areas, it cannot explain some policy decisions; for example, the decision to open economies to competition and to privatize the dominant state-owned firms. The pattern of implementation of liberal reforms can partly be explained by the different diffusion mechanisms working through interaction with international institutions, and partly by more conventional political economy explanations of interest groups and national institutions.

Global Markets and Government Regulation in Telecommunications sheds new light on old debates. First, this book highlights the importance and differential effects of the role of international organizations in the global spread of liberal policy reforms. Although many scholars assert the importance of international institutions, this is the first study to examine systematically how international institutions, in particular the World Trade Organization (WTO), the European Union (EU), and the Organization for Economic Cooperation and Development (OECD), play critical roles in the diffusion of liberal telecom reforms.

Second, this book recasts the long-standing debate over global convergence versus persistent national divergence in generating incentives and pressures for the emergence of common global standards while simultaneously creating significant space within which national governments and actors can craft autonomous policy responses. There is diversity within convergence. Thus, *Global Markets and Government Regulation in Telecommunications* is a story about common global changes with important domestic variations that go beyond "national styles of regulation" (Vogel 2006).

Third, this book bridges important literatures that too often talk past each other in assessing the current, more open global economy. Conventional political economy explanations of telecommunications policy reform focus primarily on domestic interest groups and state institutions, ignoring the importance of international organizations, international markets, and international policy diffusion (Levy and Spiller 1994; Noll and Rosenbluth 1995; Thatcher 1999). International relations scholarship focuses in general more on international organizations and member states (Checkel 2005; Finnemore 1993, 1996; Vreeland 2003), international regimes (Cowhey 1990; Sandholtz 1993), or the enduring power of nation-states (Drezner 2007; Krasner 1991), and not as much on sources of global policy diffusion. For that matter, recent literature on global policy diffusion does not take into account the specific actors, mechanisms, and channels of international organizations (Levi-Faur and Jordana 2005; Simmons, Dobbin, and Garrett 2008).

This book, by contrast, focuses on the role of international organizations in the diffusion of regulatory reform, while addressing key drivers of variation at both the international and domestic levels of analysis. In doing so, it contributes to all of these literatures and prompts us to think differently about the interplay between international and national actors and institutions.

THE PUZZLE OF GLOBALIZATION

This book focuses on the global proliferation of independent regulatory agencies in telecommunications and the concomitant spread of neoliberal policies that caused what seems, on the surface, to be a wide degree of institutional convergence across a broad range of countries. Yet, I show that, even amidst globalization, countries retained a considerable degree of autonomy in the implementation of policies. This book builds on other, older analyses of a regime for telecommunications (Cowhey 1990) and tells a truly global story using cases from Europe.[1]

The rapid and concurrent global transformation of the telecom sector presents a puzzle that conventional political economy accounts of institutional change do not and cannot explain. What is needed is a new theory of how governments respond to global pressures to create, transform, and regulate new markets and technologies, and how the international diffusion of policy ideas can affect domestic capacity for regulation and economic policy. This book proposes this theory: that international institutions influence domestic state policy action in telecommunications. And, this book not only proposes a new theory of international actor influence in telecommunications – it has even more explanatory power than current theories.

This is the puzzle: there is an emergence of potent international actors in the last two decades of the twentieth century at the same time that nations across the board are engaging in impressively similar sector-specific regulatory change. These two phenomena are connected, but, to date, the literature has not captured these dynamics. This study brings it all together.

WHY SHOULD WE CARE?

Each person is a consumer of telecommunications, from our iPhones to our laptops, and how we get access to the globalized world is affected by political compromises in how governments regulate technology and markets. How these rules are created and

[1] For an excellent reference of an emergent new regime in Africa, see Cogburn, D. L. (2003). Governing global information and communications policy: Emergent regime formation and the impact on Africa. *Telecommunications Policy* 27, 135–53.

transformed affects who gets access to the increasingly globalized world and at what cost, and these are inherently important and political questions.

I demonstrate how some major international organizations, especially the WTO, EU, and OECD, played critical roles in structuring the international diffusion of domestic policy innovations, especially the introduction of competition into previously closed markets, the establishment of separate regulatory agencies, and the introduction of private sector participation. Other new actors emerged as well, including cross-border alliances of firms and networks of regulatory agencies.

Yet, despite global shifts indicating the increasing influence of these international organizations and layers of governance, the nation-state is alive and well. This book builds on other literatures (Berger and Dore 1996; Mosley 2003; Wibbels 2005) to argue that domestic national institutions continue to play a critical role even within the larger context of globalization, Europeanization, and other regional forces.

The proliferation of international institutions and their impact has become a central question in international relations, in analyzing how and when international institutions influence national policies (Martin and Simmons 1998). Many theories focus on the extent to which international institutions interact directly in their relations with states, through either a "teaching" or "learning" capacity (Barnett and Finnemore 2004; Finnemore 1993, 1996). Much less is known about how international institutions structure an environment in which new networks of subnational actors interact (Johnston 2008; Raustiala 2002; Slaughter 2004).

Telecommunications is an ideal lens through which to analyze this story of globalization and the role of international institutions, as it is a dynamic sector with global reach at the very heart of what is known to be globalization. Telecommunications affects people, firms, and governments, and how these evolving layers of governance have arisen affects known theories and policies about both international politics and markets. This is a story about globalization and the diffusion of technology and policies, with a tension between homogeneity and uniqueness. This story is different, however, in showing diversity within convergence, particularly in the dramatic diffusion of regulatory change. All was accomplished within ten years, an astonishing pace for institutional and regulatory change.

LIBERALIZATION, MARKET-ORIENTED REFORMS, AND RELEVANT QUESTIONS

In the tradition of more careful conceptualization and measurement (Brady and Collier 2004), I use the term "liberal reform" in reference to more general movements and policies toward opening up new markets, lifting restrictions to markets that were closed, and allowing for new entrants. *Liberalization*, in turn, refers specifically to the lifting of ownership restrictions, quotas, and restrictions to entry and exit in the telecommunications sector. *Privatization* is a separate form of market-oriented reform, and is not always an actual market-oriented reform, as empirical research has shown that private monopolists often behave just as restrictively as state-owned monopolists. Furthermore, although deregulation seems to be an example of liberalization, it is not always clear that it leads to more open markets and less government control. Frequently, deregulation leads to *re-regulation*, or what Vogel has termed "freer markets, more rules" (Vogel 1996). By separating the concepts of liberalization, privatization, and re-regulation, we can achieve more analytical leverage to understand the contours of market-oriented reform within telecoms and, arguably, other sectors subject to the vagaries of the global market.

What is not clear is how such choices diffuse among disparate nations, or why one nation chooses a particular option over another. I argue that economic policy choice, particularly the decision to establish a separate regulatory authority for telecommunications, is partly conditioned on actions by other countries and by international organizations. I address two specific questions: how did these reforms travel? And how do governments and other actors learn to regulate "for competition"? These specific questions are important because how governments regulate the telecommunications sector has substantial implications for overall competitiveness in the world economy, including strategic advantages in this key market sector (Bar and Borrus 1992).

How do governments learn how to regulate "for competition"? Vogel argues that, in the 1980s, what was known as deregulation actually entailed *re-regulation*, as governments had to introduce even more rules to enforce a freer market (Vogel 1996). This dynamic was taken to the next level in the 1990s and 2000s, as governments not only had to re-regulate sector-specific regulations but also countrywide competition rules. Many economists and practitioners advocated a shift from *ex ante* regulation to a more general competition authority (Shelanski 2002). The two prime examples of countries that tried this experiment, Australia and New Zealand, later reintroduced a sectoral regulator. Rather than following these two examples, most countries around the world created new regulatory bodies for telecommunications and the information economy.

Furthermore, as outlined later in my diffusion framework, policy makers and regulators joined together in several different groupings of international organizations and regulator networks to exchange best practices for telecom regulation and competition policy. These new transnational governance actors and mechanisms exert substantial influence on the scope and substance of domestic telecom regulations.

CHAPTER 1

Understanding Global Regulatory Reform in Telecommunications

A Paradigm Shift

TELECOMMUNICATIONS: THE OLD REGIME

For much of the twentieth century, telephony was viewed as a natural monopoly within national borders. In most of the world, the telecommunications system was governed by a government-owned or -managed monopoly responsible for postal, telegraph, and telephone services (PTT), which was operated by a ministry or regulatory agency and protected from competition in services and equipment. The state was the main actor domestically and internationally (Krasner 1991). On the international front, states cut deals with other states in order to cross-subsidize areas of service and to collect rents on the lucrative long-distance market (Cowhey 1990). States engaged in negotiations over telecommunications issues in intergovernmental organizations, especially the International Telecommunications Union (ITU). Some issues included standards for frequency and spectrum allocation, numbering, and the like. States were key members of both the International Telecommunications Satellite Organization (INTELSAT) and the International Marine/Maritime Satellite (INMARSAT) organization, which governed the placement of satellites. In addition, telecommunications involves issues of national security within countries, and some even argued that having a national telecom firm served as the symbol of a truly modern economy. Zacher and Sutton argue that "any self-respecting nation owned and controlled its ... telecommunications ... industries" (Zacher and Sutton 1996).

SIGNIFICANCE AND RELEVANCE TO GLOBAL ECONOMIC PROCESSES

In general, globalization, defined as the integration of international trade and finance, has increased. Telecommunications is one of the most global markets, and the telecommunications sector can represent up to 5 percent of a country's gross domestic product (GDP) and 10 percent of gross domestic investment, for a world total telecom market revenue of more than US$1.8 trillion (World Trade Organization [WTO], 1995–2010, for 2011). As of 2011, there were more than 5.9 billion mobile-cellular subscriptions, representing a global penetration of 87 percent globally, and 79 percent in the developing world. Mobile broadband subscriptions grew 45 percent from 2008 to 2011, and outnumber fixed-broadband subscriptions (International Telecommunications Union [ITU] 2011a, 2011b, 2011c). The ITU estimates that more than one-third of the world's population is online, and 45 percent of internet users are below the age of twenty-five (ITU 2011c).

Domestically, the telecom sector is one of the key drivers in the economy, the glue that binds together firms and market participants. Demand for telecommunications services and products is high, and there are vast profits to be made in the sector. Yet, there are also large vested interests within telecommunications, particularly the state-owned enterprises that operate the networks, manufacture equipment, and provide services. Other interests include the unions and employees of these large firms.

A well-developed telecommunications infrastructure is a key component of decisions to invest in a particular country, as it determines the ease with which firms can communicate with their business partners and conduct business transactions. Furthermore, access to telecommunications and information technology has been hailed as the key to an information society, which promises to either bridge or widen the so-called digital divide, as well as the democratic deficit. Further, telecom reform is touted as a key prerequisite to sustained economic growth in developing countries because it is the key to attracting other forms of private investment. Reshaping that sector through privatization or regulation has direct implications for economic growth and competitiveness, as well as for consumer welfare in the form of price of services and equipment, access to markets, and employment possibilities in the growing sector.

Theoretically and empirically, telecom regulatory reform provides an excellent laboratory in which to explore questions about the role of government in the economy and changing patterns of intervention and regulation, as well as to examine the diffusion of institutional practices and trends in economic policies.

As mentioned previously, one of the primary assumptions about the telecom industry is that it is a natural monopoly, a justification that is central to understanding why and how governments controlled telecommunications markets for so many years. A natural monopoly exists when the total cost of a single firm serving the whole market is lower than the total cost of two or more firms (Sharkey 1982). In this case, competition would result in cost inefficiencies.

Some of the most important characteristics of these "natural monopolies" are large economies of scale relative to the level of demand and the nature of sunk costs and high fixed capital. Traditionally, it was argued that the best way to guarantee the quality provision of equipment and supply was through a single-provider monopoly, as, for example, the Bell Telephone System in the United States or the Czechoslovak Post and Telecommunications Operator.

Some of the characteristics of telecommunications markets include a high level of vertical integration and a strict division of service provisions, with tight divisions among international telephony, long-distance, and local service. Networks traditionally were owned and operated by a state-owned incumbent, which provided all forms of telephone service. The components of these networks included the international circuits, long-distance switching, and local switching, all of which culminated in the link of copper coils that connect a customer's home or office to the overall network. This "local loop" is considered a bottleneck facility, as it is difficult to build out the connection between the publicly provided network and the home or business. According to the natural monopoly justification, only one firm was best equipped to provide the most efficient and highest quality service in connecting this local loop. There were physical reasons to justify having only one provider: one set of wires, standardization of equipment, and similar arguments.

Political factors also served to reinforce some the economic assumptions of natural monopoly. In some instances, governments saw controlling communications networks as essential from the perspective of national security. In others, control had a more authoritarian domestic political intent. In still others, control was for purely fiscal reasons, as telecom sectors generated tremendous revenues for the national budget.

TECHNOLOGICAL IMPERATIVES FOR CHANGE

Sweeping technological changes during the 1980s and 1990s especially challenged some of these natural monopoly assumptions and produced an altered system of incentives and constraints for the status quo. After outlining some of these key technological changes and their specific impacts on telecom market segments in Chapters 1 and 2, I argue that technological changes are a necessary, but not sufficient, explanation for both trend and variation in telecom regulatory reform.

Some of the most important technological changes include discoveries and innovations in digital switches, microwave technology, technology for mobile phones, new advances in the broadband technology (for asymmetric digital subscriber line [ADSL], cable modems), satellite technology, and fiber-optic cable links. One of the most significant implications of advances in coaxial cable, satellites, wireless networks, and call-back technology is that it became easier to circumvent market entry barriers to providing telecoms services. Such technological changes created the possibility of substituting new services at lower prices through new companies without having to pay fees to the dominant monopoly firm. Advances in digital switching technology made it possible for several providers, not just one, to share telecommunications infrastructure. What was once technologically impossible became much cheaper and widely available (Pool and Noam 1990).

Once introduced, increased competition chipped away at the monopoly rents the dominant incumbents were able to collect. Some of the rents associated with state ownership included price discrimination between different types of consumers, especially businesses and residential users, and also price differentials among the provision of international, long-distance, and local telephone services. Traditionally, governments used the lucrative rents of high-priced international calls to cross-subsidize the provision of local service, thus distorting the overall market yet guaranteeing rents for the state operator.

Older technology and bottleneck facilities provided justification for monopolists to block any competitive entry and to maintain the rents. New technologies enhanced the ability of new entrants into market segments, especially in the areas of value-added technology, long-distance telephony, and the local loop. Many competitors praised the advent of cellular telephony as a substitute for fixed lines, as consumers no longer had to wait years, in some cases, for the state-owned incumbent to provide a line to the home. Rather, they could purchase a mobile phone with the technology to dial around the world, thus providing access to a more global information society (Castells 2007). Yet, wireless technology has emerged as a complement to, and not merely a substitute for, fixed-line telephony, particularly in terms of access to the internet and broadband. Fixed-line service through digital subscriber lines (DSL) has proven to be one of the most pervasive access points to the internet, although mobile broadband subscriptions have grown by more than 45 percent, especially in developing countries (ITU 2011c). Many scholars debate the importance of governance in the emerging areas of the internet. Mueller, for example, provides a fascinating study of how networks and states interact to form a new global politics of internet governance (Mueller 2010). I use some of these ideas in my own theoretical framework, as outlined later in this chapter and in Chapter 2.

Technology has also altered the incentives for governments to retain the previous structures of vertically integrated firms, as governments have started to introduce competition in various segments of the telecom market and spin off separate companies to provide services to these segments. Finally, the technological transformation of telecommunications further undermined natural monopoly assumptions by circumventing some of the previous geographic barriers to entry into the global communications market. For example, rural villagers in Nepal are now able to use mobile phones not only to talk to people around the world, but also to check market prices of goods and commodities and make trade arrangements by both phone and internet. The mountains of the Himalayas do not constitute the same natural barriers to global communications they once did. Furthermore, communications technology and the role of electronic commerce and e-government is not value-neutral and could pose threats to privacy, cyber-security, and other undesirable attributes. Mueller, for example, uses network theory and argues that the internet requires a different governance structure, one that includes a political movement to define, defend, and institutionalize individual rights and freedoms on a transnational scale (Mueller 2010).

WAVES OF REFORM

The liberalization of telecommunications increased and accelerated over the past two decades, and can be divided into three distinct periods or "waves" of reform. In the early 1980s, during the first wave, the dominant form of governing and regulating telecommunications was the PTT monopoly. Only the United States had private ownership and a separate regulator (since 1934), although the Bell System was still a monopoly, and there were plenty of arguments about the "regulatory capture" of the Federal Communications Commission (FCC) by the Bell companies (Stigler 1971). During this same period, however, the United Kingdom and Japan embarked on paths of substantial re-regulation in telecommunications, as well as in other sectors (Vogel 1996). The United Kingdom established a separate regulator, Oftel, to enforce competition in telecommunications (Thatcher 1999), and Japan started a program of re-regulation (Noll and Rosenbluth 1995).

The second wave of reforms in telecommunications started in Latin America, especially in Argentina, Mexico, and Chile

(Murillo 2001; Noam 1998; Petrazzini 1995; Ramamurti 1996). This wave also included countries in Eastern Europe, which began the transition from socialist economies toward market economies, and many countries began programs of large-scale economic reform, some of which involved privatizing telecommunications. In this wave of reform, the emphasis was placed mostly on privatization of the incumbent, lining state coffers and supplementing the budget, and modernizing the antiquated telecom networks. The main actors in this case were governments as they chose to corporatize state-owned monopolies, spin off a separate regulatory unit in the ministry, and prepare for privatization and eventual liberalization of the sector. In these cases, liberalization was something planned for the future – not an immediate issue. Policy-makers pursued goals of making money through selling shares of the state-owned incumbents, increasing investment in the telecom infrastructure in order to provide the capacity for modernized services, and providing more services to consumers.

The third wave included a much larger group of countries spanning even more regions of the globe. These countries included most developing countries and dynamic middle- income countries (Singapore, Hong Kong, Korea) (Fink, Mattoo, and Rathindran 2003; Singh 1999). The third wave also included countries in Europe, as well as the European Union (EU) as a whole, which started to liberalize its telecommunications sector by 1998. The main goals during later waves were to accelerate the privatization process and to continue to liberalize the sector. For example, member states of the European Union had until 1998 to fully liberalize all market segments of telecommunications, including the local loop. The year when most countries around the world established an independent regulator was 2000 (European Commission 2010a). During this time, markets were booming, and countries wanted to hop on board the investment train; however, it also became apparent that global capital was not infinite. Over the past ten years, the number of countries with competitive markets and separate regulatory institutions has increased, albeit at a slower pace.

Some of the key challenges following the "bubble" of 2000, as well as the global financial crash of 2008, included booming demand in developing countries, the erosion of shareholder value in developed country telecom markets, and the consolidation of state ownership in both incumbents and mobile telephony. In the Czech Republic, as shown later in the book, the government regained ownership of Czech Telecom after foreign investors sold out their shares, and waited several years before re-selling the firm to Telefonica of Spain. Also, with the increased digitization of technology and the "convergence" of platforms for electronic communications, countries and regulators are devising more ways to ensure effective interconnection policy with multiple networks and to provide affordable, accessible, high-quality service for citizens. Many countries have designed new broadband access strategies based on the EU's *Digital Europe Policy* (European Commission 2010a, 2010b, 2010c), and some of the new technologies raise questions about how to regulate and govern the internet, voice over internet protocol (VOIP) issues, and other technical advances in a way that might respond to the interests of citizens, states, and firms (Marsden 2011; Pelkmans and Renda 2011). Also, more recent literature shows how the position of telecommunications has moved in international organizations, shifting away from more traditional notions of telecommunications to that of information infrastructure, driven by larger debates about information rights and information governance (Avant, Finnemore, and Sell 2010; Cowhey, Aronson, and Abelson 2009). I engage some of these later arguments in the conclusion of this book, focusing on the historical spread of liberalism in the 1990s and early 2000s.

With this brief historical overview, we now turn to some of the specific trends in global reforms.

THE DEPENDENT VARIABLE: THE CREATION OF SIMILAR, LIBERAL INSTITUTIONAL INNOVATIONS IN TELECOMMUNICATIONS AROUND THE WORLD

Those governments that chose to enact regulatory reform in telecommunications have stated explicitly a set of goals to increase the accessibility, quality, and affordability of telecommunications services. The availability and affordability of modern, reliable telecommunications services are critical for all sectors in the economy, especially in order to attract foreign investment, compete in global markets, and fulfill overall development objectives. Also, telecommunications has proved to be correlated with economic growth and development, and it has come to be understood as one of the fundamental building blocks of a modern economy (Röller and Waverman 2001).

One of the biggest challenges for regulators – and for governments when devising their actual policies – is how to retain the flexibility to grapple with the challenges of rapidly changing technology but still maintain a firm set of guidelines to ensure transparent, effective, and market-enhancing rules. Given the very real costs and benefits, the entrenched interests of the incumbent firms, and the high stakes for investment, all countries around the world face these tough challenges.

Telecommunications markets have opened considerably over the past three decades. The bulk of liberalizations happened in the late 1990s, the bulk of privatizations occurred in the mid-1990s, and the highest period of activity in the establishment of separate regulators and re-regulation occurred in the late 1990s and early 2000s. By 2001, more than 120 governments had established separate regulatory agencies for telecoms, more than 100 governments had introduced private sector participation into the dominant fixed-line operator, and more than 100 governments had introduced liberalization in at least one market segment. In terms of re-regulation, more than 106 countries established interconnection frameworks, and more than 50 percent of countries around the world had established a fund for universal service (ITU 2011a). By 2011, 158 countries had established separate regulatory institutions, 126 had some form of private sector participation, and over 140 countries established a regulatory framework for dispute resolution, up from seventy in 2005 (ITU 2011a, 2011b, 2011c). In addition, more than seventy governments adopted a policy for broadband access (ITU 2011a, 2011b, 2011c).

ESTABLISHING A NEW, SEPARATE TELECOM REGULATORY AGENCY

From 1980 to 2002, there was a tremendous global movement to adopt new, separate telecommunications regulators. In the early 1980s, most countries had a state-owned monopoly telecommunications operator, and the government ministry responsible for communications usually performed regulatory duties, as well as ownership and management duties. By 2002, more than 129 countries had created separate regulators for telecoms, and 106 countries had at least partially privatized their monopoly incumbent telecommunications operators (see Appendix A).

Appendix B illustrates the cumulative adoption of separate regulators for telecoms from 1934 (the creation of the U.S. FCC) through 2011. These figures show only nine separate regulators in 1980, but more than 158 by 2011, with an upward sloping curve starting in the 1990s.

WHAT IS A SEPARATE REGULATOR?

By late 2001, more countries had established separate regulatory bodies for telecoms than had private participation in basic infrastructure or that permitted competition in basic services. This number increased to 158 countries by 2010. Establishing a separate regulator for telecoms can be viewed as one step toward an overall paradigm shift from a state-owned, -controlled, and -regulated telecom sector to a more market-oriented competitive sector. This new institution is crucial for regulating a dynamic, global sector, especially as governments introduce competition into previously closed market segments and begin to privatize the incumbent, which usually retains a significant degree of market power. A survey from the European Bank of Reconstruction and Development (EBRD) in 1995 indicated that,

> "the absence of an independent regulatory authority to establish the rules of the game, arbitrate disputes, and generally determine the public interest is a danger signal to potential investors. It has been demonstrated many times over that investors are much more

comfortable with a privatization offer that involves an independent regulatory authority"

(European Bank for Reconstruction and Development [EBRD] 1995).

Some scholars have compared arguments for the establishment of independent regulatory agencies for telecoms with similar arguments about the importance of having independent central banks. There are two important similarities between having independent telecom regulators and independent central banks, and two key differences. The first similarity is that the logic of having an independent regulator or an independent central bank will ensure a degree of distance from short-term, politically motivated government attempts to intervene actively in the formulation of important policies. In the case of telecoms, this means the daily operation of key communication networks, infrastructures, and services; for banks, it means the creation and enactment of monetary policy. The second similarity is the importance of signaling to the market, both domestic and international, that the government is committed to upholding particular policy goals without political interference. Thus, there are both direct effects of intervening in the market, and indirect effects by signaling intentions to the broader investment community.

The differences, however, are important. First, in the case of central banks, it is arguably easier to observe when a government is meddling with monetary policy as a public policy tool than it is in the case of telecom regulation, which is a much more opaque process and is less clearly related to highly observable economic outcomes. Second, the stakeholders are different. In the case of telecommunications, the interest groups in favor of status quo protection and active government participation in the market are much more deeply committed and entrenched, and the potential beneficiaries are much more diffuse and sometimes less politically active. Also, many of the regulatory interventions have been challenged in the courts and are often held up for years due to the accompanying tangle of legislative and juridical processes and precedents.

The establishment of a regulatory office separate from the incumbent was first seen as a corollary to its privatization. It first became necessary to create a separate regulatory office as the state began to divest itself from management of the PTT and sought to attract private investment. But, later in the process, it became even clearer that the government needed to create a regulatory office separate from the policy-making arm of government, particularly a new ministry for telecoms or informatics.

Having a separate regulator was no longer enough to demonstrate a credible commitment to private investors or to do the complex work of regulating a dynamic market sector. This was partly a functionalist need, but also the result of a policy network in which this complex idea became internalized in the minds of elites through the channels of international organizations, agencies, and networks of policy experts. I show in Chapters 2, 4, and 5 how the complex idea of liberal, market-oriented reforms in telecommunications spread through these very channels of policy networks.

Establishing a new, separate, and independent regulator for telecommunications usually involves several steps. Under the previous telecommunications regulatory regime, most governments owned, operated, and regulated the PTT company. The largest exception was the FCC in the United States, which was established as an independent regulatory authority in 1934 (Page 1941).

One of the first steps in reforming the market for telecommunications involved creating a new corporate entity for the PTT (corporatization), to prepare it for possible privatization, and separating the regulatory unit from the incumbent operator. This often involved creating a separate regulatory office within the ministry for transport and communications. The office thus was separate from the incumbent, but not from the ministry. The next step often included the formation of a separate telecom office outside the ministry, complete with separate financing, a budget, and an appointment process. However, this evolution is not a linear process, and countries demonstrate a range of actual independence for the separate regulator itself. For example, as shown later in the book, many of the Nordic countries have had a regulatory agency separate from the operations of telecommunications, and these are regarded as independent although still housed within a ministry. Thus, multiple independent regulatory options are possible, although many countries choose an agency model.

One definition of a separate regulator is included within the World Trade Organization (WTO) Basic Agreement on Telecommunications Services, and the accompanying Reference Paper: "The regulatory body is separate from, and not accountable to, any supplier of basic telecommunications services. The decisions of and the procedures used by regulators shall be impartial with respect to all market participants" (WTO 1995–2010). Another definition of a "separate regulator" is in place when a country has established a regulator separate from both the incumbent telecom operator and the relevant government ministry (usually transport and communications), and the regulator is independent in terms of finance and authority.

Establishing a separate regulator for telecoms is an example of liberalization that is extremely difficult to implement. In trade and finance, it is possible to introduce some liberal reform by lifting price controls and tariffs. Introducing a new regulatory institution, however, generates a realm of complexity in both form and substance. The creation of the institution itself requires new laws to be adopted by the national legislature, including the adoption of parallel legislation for the actual telecom law that affects the national budget, competition law, and myriad other policies (e.g., power of newly privatized firms to expropriate private property for new facilities). In terms of substance, a separate regulatory institution requires a level of economic, regulatory, and specific telecommunications expertise and knowledge to handle policy questions of tariff rebalancing, universal service objectives, interconnection policy, and distribution of scarce resources (e.g., spectrum, numbering plans).

A government that wants to introduce competition into a previously closed economy also wants to have an institution to monitor and enforce this competition. Yet, it is not evident that a "separate" or "independent" regulator is the only possible option, let alone the best option. Countries have vastly different starting points in terms of basic levels of development and infrastructure, market competition, experience of incumbents and firms, and attractiveness for investment. Moreover, governments vary widely in their institutional endowments, capacity for regulation in general, and telecom regulatory capacity in particular. Even advanced industrial countries thus far have had little experience with separate regulatory authorities for telecoms, and regulatory effectiveness is still questioned from all political sides, even in some of the more experienced countries (e.g., the United States and the United Kingdom), where some observers complain of "regulatory capture" by firms whereas others call for tougher regulation. Furthermore, the regulator needs to be able to regulate not only the incumbent and others with significant market power (SMP), but must also be able to withstand considerable public scrutiny and legal battles over its decisions. Regulators also play a role in terms of interaction with other governments within regulatory networks. Slaughter writes that "regulators are the new diplomats on the frontline of issues that were once the exclusive preserve of domestic policy but that cannot be resolved by national authorities alone" (Slaughter 2004). Other scholars who have studied the emergence of regulatory agencies include Gilardi on regulatory agencies in Europe (Gilardi 2008), and Maggetti (2009) and Thatcher (2007).

Given the difficulty and complexity of establishing a separate regulator, it becomes even more of a puzzle that more than 158 countries around the world have adopted separate regulators, particularly within such a short time period. Creating these new bodies for regulating competitive markets was one tool in an overall strategy of market liberalization, especially in telecommunications. The next section discusses some of the main principles and premises of telecom regulation, and how the institution of separate regulatory agencies interacts with policy-makers, firms, and alternative operators.

LIBERALIZATION OF TELECOM REGULATION

Liberalization refers to lifting entry requirements into market segments and removing barriers to licensing for services. The telecommunications market is segmented, and most countries liberalized value-added services first. Most countries preserved monopoly rights of the incumbent at least through 1998, and usually through 2003, particularly in the area of voice telephony, international services, long-distance, and the "final mile" or local loop, which refers to the last segment that connects the network to the home or business. Newer market segments include wireless local loops, ADSL, cable, fixed wireless broadband, satellites, internet services, and international gateways (ITU 2010). Most countries liberalized markets for cellular mobile telephony, the internet, and leased-line services, followed by long-distance calls, international calls, and local service. By 2010, more than 90 percent of the world had competitive markets in mobile communications (ITU 2010).

Lifting barriers to entry and removing hurdles to license restrictions, however, are only steps toward the development of competitive markets. Competition may be legally permitted, but the actual development of competition is more difficult. For example, although some African countries authorized competition in cable television, many of these countries did not have even a single cable television operator. Furthermore, even some of the most liberalized markets in advanced industrial countries have local markets that continue to be dominated by an incumbent telecommunications operator with SMP.

Re-regulation is the introduction of new sectoral regulations specifically for the telecommunications sector. It includes creating and introducing new competition rules for newly liberalized telecommunications environments, as well as new legislation and regulation involving the resolution of interconnection,[1] the development and implementation of universal service provisions,[2] and the creation of dispute settlement arrangements and transparent procedures for defining actors with SMP.

[1] *Interconnection* refers to the physical connection of separate telephone networks to allow users of those networks to communicate with each other. Interconnection ensures interoperability of services and increases end users' choice of network operators and service providers.

[2] *Universal Service Obligations,* or Universal Access Obligations, refer to the availability, nondiscriminatory access, and widespread affordability of telephone service. The level of universal service traditionally has been measured statistically as a percentage of households with a telephone.

PRIVATIZATION

The second major form of liberal telecom reform is the privatization of the state-owned telecommunications operator. Over the past twenty years, countries around the world have been privatizing state-owned firms at a tremendous pace, with revenues from privatizations estimated to be close to US$1 trillion through 1999 (Megginson and Netter 2001). Privatization generally refers to the transfer of ownership from the public sector to variants of private sector ownership (Vickers and Yarrow 1988). Privatization can range from full, 100 percent private ownership to variations of state management and control through direct shares, portfolio shares, voting rights, and leasing arrangements. In most countries, the privatization of the state-owned incumbent signals an important shift from the previous mode of telecommunications governance.

More than seventy countries introduced some degree of private sector participation in their predominantly state-owned incumbent telecom operators during the 1990s. By the end of 2001, 106 incumbents had at least partial private sector ownership, whereas eighty-three remained fully state-owned. As of 2010, as stated earlier, 126 countries had partly or fully privatized their telecom operator (ITU 2011c).

One of the key trends in private-sector participation in global telecoms is the emergence of large global strategic alliances, cross-border ownership, and changing configurations of investor partnerships. Vodafone, for example, is one of the world's largest mobile cellular operators and has invested in mobile cellular and fixed-line networks in many countries with local subsidiaries.[3] Some incumbent fixed-line carriers, such as France Télécom, Deutsche Telekom, and Telefonica (Spain), have invested in fixed-line, mobile, and broadband markets in Europe, Africa, and the Americas. In Asia, Singapore's Singtel has operations and investments in more than twenty countries, with hubs in Singapore and Australia.[4]

[3] http://www.vodafone.co.uk

[4] http://www.singtel.com

DOMESTIC POLITICS: ECONOMIC THEORY AND COMPARATIVE POLITICAL ECONOMY

Theories of regulation traditionally focus on domestic political and economic determinants of regulatory change. Economic theories of regulation are based on one-country models of government intervention in markets where monopolists hold SMP in areas of market failure (Peltzman 1976; Stigler 1971). These theories usually start with a domestic market failure and the presence of a domestic monopolist, often in strategic infrastructure. In a world with no information or transactions costs, governments that maximize social welfare, and well-defined and enforceable property rights, markets will achieve efficient outcomes (Coase 1960). These concentrated interest-group pressures produce distortionary effects in policy making, as shown in the economic literature on rent-seeking (Krueger 1974). Put simply, when markets are imperfect, Adam Smith's "invisible hand" will not work (Pigou 1938).

It is useful to look at some of the standard texts on regulation to examine the received wisdom of how markets work. Laffont and Tirole's text, one of the more contemporary on competition in telecommunications, contains theoretical models within one country (Laffont and Tirole 2000). Other economic texts present changes in telecommunications markets, but focus less on exogenous shock and more on policy response within a one-country model (Viscusi, Vernon, and Harrington 2000). There are not many accounts of "open economy" micro-economics and regulation, nor are there theoretical accounts of external actors involved in creating the regulatory shifts.

Other economists proclaim that regulation failure is much greater than market failure, since regulators cannot truly know the costs of what they're regulating. Furthermore, why should some of these *ex ante* regulations know better than a market clearing mechanism? Companies will always have the incentive to withhold information from regulators (thus creating information asymmetry), and this places too much of a burden on regulators, who cannot possibly know better than the market (Hahn 2000; Kahn 2001). Government intervention in general is seen as a failure of regulation, and the creation of new regulations and regulatory institutions is even more catastrophic for those who believe in the folklore of deregulation (Cudahy 1998).

Powerful interest groups lobby national governments for regulatory "reform," defined in this instance as policy changes that open up, deregulate, or privatize previously controlled or regulated telecom sectors. Pro-reform actors in telecommunications can include those who would benefit from such reforms; namely, alternative telecommunications service providers, companies other than the dominant incumbent or mobile phone firm, internet service providers, some large business users of services (e.g., financial services firms), and perhaps consumer organizations. Anti-reform actors often include equipment manufacturers, incumbent monopolists, labor unions, and those who would lose if telecommunications is deregulated or if competition is introduced. According to this logic, we might expect to see variation in telecom reform outcomes due to variation in the strengths of interest groups across countries.

Yet, many studies have shown mixed results in the effects of privatization on interest groups that were supposed to be the losers of such a redistribution. Teichman and Schamis found that industrial and financial conglomerates were some of the biggest winners in privatization in Latin America (Schamis 2002; Teichman 2001). Further, Murillo showed that labor unions received government concessions to win support for privatization and market-opening policies in Latin America (Murillo 2001). Interest group pressure is real and important, yet I argue that it is not possible to read preferences off interest groups. Even if big interests are represented in telecommunications, the adoption of liberal, market-oriented reform flows from state-led regulatory reform, informed by the global spread of ideas and ideology of governments and markets, and spreads through the channels of international organizations and networks.

Also, the boundaries of what can be considered international and what is domestic have become much more opaque, forcing us to look to other types of explanations. This can be interpreted through the lens of *complex interdependence* – how actors on multiple levels of analysis influence each other and the institutions within which they interact (Keohane and Nye 1977).

Much of the literature on the political economy of telecommunications reform tends to focus either on policy-makers who make decisions at times of crisis, usually in terms of balance of payments, debt, or some other economic shock (Bates and Krueger 1993), or on the performance of the sector in question. Some studies have shown that poor sectoral performance was associated with market-oriented reforms in Latin American telecommunications (Petrazzini 1995). Policy-makers choose among relatively well-known policy alternatives, and the political economy literature tends to focus on why they choose one response versus others, and why any response is so often suboptimal. In this view, politics is the problem because it is conceptualized in the literature as the competition for resources among self-interested individual actors, a distortion of markets, rather than contested interests of legitimate policy groups. Politics in this sense is conceptualized as an obstacle to the enactment of "rational" economic policies.

Other analyses of telecommunications base their models in the new institutional economics (North 1990), yet provide a more comparative approach to divergent responses to market conditions. Levy and Spiller wrote a classic work on how political institutions are important for economic performance, which was extended in quantitative analysis in later years (Levy and Spiller 1996; Li and Xu 2002). Levy and Spiller argued that a country's institutional endowments at the level of macro-politics affected the scope of arbitrary government intervention and investor confidence about asset appropriation, which in turn affected economic performance in the telecommunications sector. Some of these institutions, they emphasized, included the existence of an independent judiciary, unified or divided governments (presidential or parliamentary systems), and regulatory bureaucracy (Levy and Spiller, 1994, 1996).

Witold Henisz built upon some of these hypotheses and conducted a series of studies on the role of political constraints, a system of checks and balances, in determining outcomes in telecommunications and infrastructure investment (Henisz 2000). Henisz and Zelner found that political constraints showed a strong and positive relationship to the growth of telephone main lines per capita in a study of 147 countries from 1960 to 1994 (Henisz and Zelner 2001). I test some of these hypotheses in Chapters 2 and 3, while also introducing the importance of international organizations as a key explanatory variable of telecom regulatory reform.

Traditional comparative political economy analyses show how countries respond independently to external shocks in the global economy and how policy change differs according to domestic political and economic interests and institutions (Frieden and Rogowski 1996; Gourevitch 1986; Katzenstein 1985; Keohane and Milner 1996). Yet, these analyses have difficulties explaining why so many countries with different political and economic configurations, partisan politics, and interest concentrations adopted similar institutions in the form of separate regulatory authorities for telecoms.

Other scholars focus more on the historical paths of market types and emphasize that liberal, Anglo-Saxon countries (e.g., the United States and the United Kingdom) are definitely leaders and first movers in telecom regulatory reform. Yet, the "varieties of capitalism" arguments (Hall and Soskice 2001) that predict divergence fail to explain the common trend of establishing these separate regulators, especially in statist France and corporatist Germany (Schmidt 2002).

Still other scholars stress the importance of the partisan leanings of government and the ideological bases for economic reform (Garrett 1998). Governments dominated by right-wing parties often espouse liberal economic programs, including deregulation, liberalization, privatization, and the introduction of competition. Many of these efforts are rooted in an ideological commitment to "roll back" the role of the government in the economy, as well as in more pro-business and pro-market policies in general. I test some of these hypotheses in the econometric analysis in Chapter 3, as well as in the case studies, in Chapters 4 and 5. Many studies of Organization for Economic Cooperation and Development (OECD) economies have concluded that the party orientation of the ruling coalition affects the likelihood that countries would adopt Keynesianism (Hall 1993), and Boix argues that privatization is one example of policy differences between conservative and socialist parties in the OECD (Boix 1998). These explanations would predict substantial variation across countries according to partisan orientation in the government, and would predict that right-wing parties would be more likely to enact liberal regulatory reform, particularly by establishing separate and independent regulators. I test these hypotheses in Chapters 3, 4, and 5.

Adopting liberal reform has desirable economic effects. Deregulation, privatization, and liberalization increase the performance quality of public utilities (D'Souza and Megginson 1999). Fink et al. found that a combination of the creation of an independent regulator, privatization, and market liberalization is associated with higher levels of mainline telephones per 100 people, as well as with higher productivity than in nonreforming countries (Fink et al. 2003). Wallsten's study of thirty countries in Africa and Latin America showed that privatization increased performance, especially when combined with the creation of a new telecom regulator separate from the incumbent operator (Wallsten 2001). Others have found that privatization can produce efficiency gains when accompanied by liberalization in telecommunications in Latin America (Gutierrez and Berg 2000). In a more recent study, Waverman uses ITU data to construct a "regulatory governance index," designed to assess the actual impact of regulations and regulatory index (Waverman and Koutroumpis 2011); this index shows great variation across countries in the effects of liberal telecommunications.[5]

Why the Sudden Rush to Change?

These arguments may help explain an individual country's decisions to liberalize, but it is far more difficult to pinpoint the exact crisis or trigger that would cause more than 158 countries to

[5] In a future study, it would be desirable to use this index to test some of the hypotheses advanced in this book.

establish separate regulators over the course of ten years, or to adopt such wide-ranging means of reform. Although the crisis hypothesis can be tested in the econometric overview, as well as in the cases, a preliminary glance does not reveal a consistent pattern of deficit, debt, or financial crisis that could explain either the trend in liberal reforms or the variation in the implementation of these reforms. Yet, the possibility of a worldwide crisis that could provoke a global trend in telecoms reforms suggests the possibility of other international and external pressures for liberal reform – that of international policy diffusion.

Another possible explanation for the spread of liberal telecom reform is the increasing interconnectedness of the global market economy and society. The literature on globalization is voluminous, and I draw selectively upon some of the key predictions in order to formulate hypotheses for how globalization might affect telecom regulatory reform. Some scholars argue that states embrace neoliberal policies for reasons of achieving or maintaining competitiveness in a globalizing world (Cerny 1995; Grunberg 1998; Strange 1996). Globalization is sometimes framed as a fight between states and markets, or as an evil that causes social dislocation and undermines state sovereignty and developmental goals (Rudra 2002; Stiglitz 2002). In the case of telecom regulatory reform, globalization plays a role by opening domestic economies to the vagaries of the international market and to the whims and follies of global investors. We might predict that globalization, as defined by increased integration in international trade and finance, would lead to convergence in liberal telecom regulatory reform. And yet, it is unclear how globalization may actually affect policy outcomes – one analytical tool to determine this question is global policy diffusion.

DIFFUSION

One key missing piece of the puzzle in explaining the striking trend in liberal telecom reform is the role of international policy diffusion or interdependent decision making among countries, in which the policy choice of one country is conditioned on the prior actions of other countries. In recent years, a growing literature on "policy diffusion" has emerged to explain the adoption and spread of institutions and policies around the world. Multiple definitions of diffusion abound, and these range from extremely broad definitions, such as, "the spread of something within a social system" (Strang and Soule 1998) to narrower definitions such as, "the process by which an innovation is communicated through certain channels over time among the members of a social system" (Rogers 1995).

Following the example of others, I use the term *diffusion* to refer to all processes in which "prior adoption of a trait or practice in a population alters the probability of adoption for remaining non-adopters" (Strang 1991). Diffusion of policies is a kind of information-generating process, a growing literature of which focuses on some of these broad trends toward liberalization around the world, including the diffusion of policy choices in the areas of political liberalism (Simmons, Dobbin, and Garrett 2006), democracy (Brinks and Coppedge 2006), constitutions (Elkins, Ginsburg, and Melton 2009), markets and democracy (Simmons, Dobbin, and Garrett 2008), pension reform (Brooks 2009; Orenstein 2008), regulatory capitalism and utilities (Levi-Faur 2005; Levi-Faur and Jordana 2005), and other utilities (Henisz, Zelner, and Guillen 2005). This literature in turn builds on work on the diffusion of innovations across American states, including institutional innovations (Walker 1969), education (Gray 1973; Mintrom 1997), and tax innovations (Berry and Berry 1992).

Some of these scholars of diffusion have focused on the spread of independent regulatory agencies in Europe (Gilardi 2005, 2008; Lazer 2001; Thatcher 2002) and also in Latin America (Jordana and Levi-Faur 2006; Weyland 2006). Others have focused on comparative case research in the United States and Europe (Héritier, Knill, and Mingers 1996; Lazer and Mayer-Schönberger 2002). I build on some of these studies to focus on global diffusion of regulatory innovations in telecommunications, using a systematic and empirical analysis in Chapter 3, as well as more fine-grained case studies in Chapters 4 and 5. Some of the diffusion literature does not include a specification of actors and pathways through which these reforms could travel, and this book fills in the gaps of this exciting literature.

To restate the argument, it is international organizations interacting with domestic states that are primary drivers of policy convergence in the important arena of telecommunications and in ways that are perhaps surprising. These organizations play a critical role in three ways: they create preferences for reform, they shape the preferences for reform, and they provide forums for expert discussions and the emergence of policy standards, which are often rooted in an underlying ideology of liberalism. Yet, these forces for international policy convergence also leave room for substantial variation among countries, showing the enduring power of states and domestic political institutions in accelerating, accepting, or resisting reform, as well as in the specific tailoring of institutions within domestic political and economic climates.

This book first introduces a theoretical framework to explain why, when, and how countries choose to enact market-oriented reform in telecommunications, particularly in the establishment of separate regulatory authorities, but also in the liberalization of market segments and privatization of the dominant telecommunications firm. Chapter 2 focuses on the role of three channels of diffusion through international organizations – information, harmonization, and networks – and provides examples of how these organizations may play a role in the domestic institutional innovations in countries around the world.

Next, Chapter 3 tests several hypotheses from the theoretical framework and asks when and why countries choose to establish separate regulators and privatize incumbent telecom operators. Using a Weibull multivariate hazard model, this chapter analyzes the timing of establishing a separate regulator and privatizing the telecom incumbent in 184 countries from 1975 to 2001. The main findings are that (1) membership in international organizations, especially the WTO and the OECD, plays a critical role in explaining the timing of the creation of separate regulators; (2) a country's debt service affects its probability of liberal telecom reform, in that the higher the debt service, the more likely the country will be to establish a separate regulator, perhaps through two mechanisms of pressure from international institutions and as a signal to future private investors; (3) a country's political configuration, especially the number of veto points in the domestic polity as measured by the Political Constraints index, has a positive association with the timing of telecom reform; and (4) although some explicit tests of diffusion were examined, several common measures for general diffusion did not have much explanatory power, showing the elusive nature of this underlying process.

It seems clear that ideas and technology are diffusing around the world and creating new opportunities and constraints for policy, but, in the case of telecommunications, these variables (as popularly measured in the literature) do not have much explanatory power. Rather, diffusion is more embedded in other forms of explanation of the timing of reform, namely the importance and influence of international institutions in the production and spread of ideas and best practices, the creation of incentives and constraints to modify the status quo, and the changing patterns of domestic interests. It becomes even more necessary to examine the actors and mechanisms in these processes of policy change, as shown in Chapters 4 and 5.

The contrast of Central and Eastern Europe (CEE) with Northern Europe is particularly poignant, in that the CEE countries tried to "return to Europe" through the introduction of liberal market economies and democracies. They followed the loose guidelines and overall ideological stance of liberalism, which was preached not only by the EU, which they sought to join, but also by other rich "country club" organizations (e.g., the OECD and the WTO). Furthermore, some of the biggest and most influential think tanks and policy research organizations, as well as those providing funds (e.g., the World Bank and the International Monetary Fund), followed a similar ideological commitment in promoting reforms, as will be shown in the coming chapters. The Northern European countries, however, followed some aspects of liberalization but in their own social democratic style.

Chapters 4 and 5 analyze countries that are now part of the New Europe, the EU-25. In Chapter 4, I analyze the case of middle-income countries that recently joined the EU to test specifically the hypotheses of external drivers of policy change. Membership in the EU and also membership in the OECD played an important role in introducing the language and concepts of reform, as well as the shape of the eventual regulators. The case examples of Hungary, the Czech Republic, Poland, and Slovakia illustrate the similarities of reform (timing of establishing separate regulators) and the comprehensiveness of reform (all made efforts to liberalize, privatize, and establish separate regulators). Yet, these countries retain country and sectoral characteristics that cannot be reduced to strictly outside-in arguments. These countries continue to display national patterns of divergence within this overall liberal trend, conditional on some interactions with international organizations, as well as with key domestic political influences, including political leadership, patterns of state control in the economy, the role of the state, and business–government relations.

Chapter 5 analyzes small, high-income countries in Northern Europe. Although case selection proceeded according to income groups and country size in order to provide a controlled comparison with the other countries of Eastern Europe, it turns out that all four countries of Northern Europe (the Netherlands, Denmark, Sweden, and Finland) are known to be innovators and leaders in telecom liberalization, although in different ways. The chapter outlines some key trends in liberal reforms, especially the interaction of market and international institutions, and then shows how the specific interaction with international organizations often helps explain the persistent variation across countries. Next, the chapter provides a comparison of these four country case examples. Even in highly competitive markets, there is considerable leeway for countries to enact their own distinctive policy choices. For example, there is great variation across these countries in the separate regulatory agency, and, although telecom firms are highly competitive, there is considerable variation in state ownership. Although Denmark fully privatized TeleDanmark and the Netherlands partially privatized KPN, the Swedes and the Finns retain considerable state ownership in their incumbent telecom operators, Telia-Sonera. Finally, the Scandinavian countries in particular stress the importance of social responsibility and consensus building, factors that are written into the mission statements of each of the separate regulatory offices, suggesting what some argue is a "Nordic model of governance" (OECD 2003b).

The concluding chapter shows how analyzing telecommunications regulatory reform helps answer key empirical questions with implications for theories of international relations and political economy, and also with policy implications for how governments around the world respond to technological change and provide access to the global information society.

Again, we are all consumers of globalization through telecommunications – our access to the world can be held in our hands. And, how this happens depends on a rich, multilayered, emerging pattern of global governance. This book tells the story of policy diffusion in one sector, yet has vast implications for global governance, as well as for forces for decentralization, fragmentation, and the enduring role of the nation-state.

CHAPTER 2

Why Change the Rules?

Explaining Liberal Telecom Reform

In a 2000 presentation on "trade in telecommunications services" to the House Commerce Subcommittee on Telecommunications, Trade, and Consumer Protection, Ambassador Richard W. Fisher, Deputy United States Trade Representative said

> Peer pressure by liberalizing countries has created a virtuous circle where countries now compete for global investment by offering more attractive investment opportunities and more effective regulatory regimes. For example, even after entry into force of the WTO Basic Telecom Agreement, Singapore, Korea, Japan and India have unilaterally decided to improve foreign investment and telecom regimes, and many EU and Latin American countries are substantially reducing interconnection rates.
>
> (Fisher 2000)

Fisher's comments point to a dramatic shift taking place over the previous decade in the shape of telecommunications provision throughout the world. Why did this happen? This chapter sets up the remainder of the book by discussing the particulars of telecom regulatory reform. The first part presents an introduction and an analytical framework to explain telecom regulatory reform. This presents an overall framework of international regulatory networks, a specific account of international organizations in telecommunications, and country-level variation and divergence. The second part presents hypotheses that flow from this theoretical framework, both main hypotheses and some alternatives. The third part presents a research design to test these hypotheses and to lay out a plan for the rest of the book. Appendix C presents the basic argument in diagram form.

Globalization and external stimuli present common forces for change in three ways – marketplaces, exported deregulation, and macroeconomic trends. *Marketplace changes*, shown through the advances of technology, as well as a promise of investment and revenues (or losses), exert strong pressure to respond; these changes apply to dynamic sectors in all countries. *Exported deregulation*, particularly from the United States and United Kingdom, exerts medium pressure to respond on all sectors and to all countries, but some more than others. For example, countries that have closer relations with the United States and the United Kingdom, as well as those that have more advanced and industrialized markets and those in the process of economic transition to market economies, might be more susceptible than countries with mono-exporting sectors (e.g., developing countries), but also perhaps than countries with a long history of social-welfare states (e.g., countries of northern Europe). *Macroeconomic trends* also present a common force for change and exert weak pressure to respond that allies to all sectors and all economies, although not all respond. In telecommunications, this can be seen in the global recession and how it affects investment and consumption patterns.

These three common forces for change then travel through global diffusion channels, via international organizations, in the form of information networks, harmonization networks, and regulator networks. *Information networks* exert weak pressure to respond via peer pressure and exchange of information and best practices, and these networks affect all countries, some more than others. The mechanisms of these networks are emulation, mimesis, and learning. Examples of actors within telecommunications networks include the International Telecommunications Union (ITU), the World Bank (WB), and the Organization for Economic Cooperation and Development (OECD).

Harmonization networks exert a strong pressure to respond and use membership conditionality and other coercive measures to ensure that countries meet common requirements and standards. These networks affect some countries more than others – both those that seek membership and some current members – and the mechanisms at work here are mimesis, emulation, and coercion. Examples of actors in telecommunications include the World Trade Organization (WTO) and the European Union (EU), with their membership conditionality and dispute settlement capabilities.

The last form of global diffusion channels through international organizations are *regulator networks* themselves. For members, these regulator networks exert a strong pressure to respond and utilize peer pressure to exchange best practices, conditionality and coercive measures, and other information-sharing measures. The mechanisms include mimesis, emulation, competition, and coercion. Some actors in regulator networks include the Body of European Regulators for Electronic Communications, the International Regulators Group, and Regulatel.

The dependent variable in all this includes specific national responses, including domestic institutional innovation in establishing separate regulatory agencies for telecommunications, privatizing the incumbent telecom operator (or not), introducing competition into various market segments and sectors, and enacting domestic legislation. The general trends, as shown above, reveal that most countries adopted some form of a separate regulatory agency for telecommunications and introduced some competition into domestic markets. Most have enacted new legislation for telecommunications and electronic communications, and many, but not all, introduced private sector participation into the main telecom incumbent. Yet, the particular mixture and the effectiveness of the policies, as well as the style of regulatory regimes, still reflect enduring national characteristics. Some of these include political leadership, the dominant attitude toward foreign investment, the type of state control, and government–business relations.

THEORETICAL CONTEXT

Many standard economic theories start with the individual as the prime unit of analysis, with assumptions about the individual and his or her tendency to barter, truck, and exchange. What they fail to include are aspects of the society in which individuals are embedded. As argued by some scholars, a market economy can only exist in a market society, and a market society must be protected against the vagaries of the market (Polanyi 1957). Regarding the diffusion of regulatory reform in telecoms, this is a return to some of the principles of markets writ large – international markets, liberalization, deregulation, and the role of the state. What is missing from many economic theories, as well as from political theories, is a dynamic model of change that incorporates the nexus between economy and society, particularly that of politics and the articulation of interests, power, and purpose.

On a deeper theoretical level, patterns and processes of communication and control are central to all systems, including political systems (Deutsch 1966). I present an international political system in which the diffusion of regulatory reform in telecommunications is one of the patterns and processes of communication and control. As I trace out some of these patterns and processes, I show some systemic changes of the system (positive feedback) and some changes within the system (negative feedback), as Deutsch outlined at an international rather than domestic level of politics (Deutsch 1966). One of these key components is the role of regulatory networks and socialization through international organizations, an issue that has been, thus far, understudied in the area of regulatory reform, especially in telecommunications.

DIFFUSION THROUGH INTERNATIONAL ORGANIZATIONS

International policy diffusion emerges not from the ether or from price signals beaming in from the outer market, but rather from people, international organizations, and social networks. Policy innovations travel through specific pathways, especially through international organizations and networks. It is possible to conceive of an international system of emulation and competition. Nation states are grouped into regions based on geography and their place in specialized sets of communication channels, through which flow new ideas, information, and policy cues. This international set of communications transmits the sets of norms and international standards for administration, and links together research institutes, national associations of professionals, international interest groups, and voluntary associations into an increasingly complex network that connects pioneering countries with more peripheral countries (Walker 1969).

My framework builds on the literature that explains policy convergence by the exchange of information among members of the same communications networks (Bennett 1991). Four of these diffusion channels are networks of information, networks for harmonization, networks of regulators themselves, and networks of firms, which builds on Slaughter's framework for analyzing transgovernmental actors (Slaughter 2004).

Information networks are designed to address a set of national and global problems, particularly those that benefit from regulation by information, dialogue, and collective learning rather than through more traditional command and control techniques. Slaughter writes that "self-regulation in the collective context means setting standards collectively and pooling information in ways that can help all participants. It is the Weight Watchers model of global governance" (Slaughter 2004: 169). This concept of information networks can be applied to telecom regulation by analyzing the international networks in which governmental and nongovernmental actors participate, particularly international institutions. Some of these international organizations influence decision-makers through the dissemination of research and intellectual debate.

Policy diffusion through *harmonization networks* occurs when countries have incentives to harmonize their telecom regulations and institutions as part of an overall shift to the adoption of common standards and harmonization within a larger telecom regime. The key difference between these organizations and the information networks is the power relations that exist between the international organization and the member states who harmonize their domestic regulations, as well as the potential for enforcement in the case of noncompliance in harmonizing regulations and institutions.

Horizontal regulatory networks are a new governance network and present a way for decision-makers within states to exchange information horizontally, in a more decentralized way. They symbolize how regulators need to exchange information on a regional level, closely linked with regional trade patterns, to exchange best practices and norms for governing and regulating the behavior of global market players and to ensure the objective of ensuring affordable access to information technology at a reasonable price to the greatest number of people.

Although not a new phenomenon, the reach of multinational telecommunications providers from within their home country market monopolies to other countries can be characterized as another type of horizontal diffusion network, a *horizontal network of firms*. For example, when Deutsche Telekom of Germany invested in Slovakia and Hungary, among other countries, it implemented many of the same kinds of policies in the host countries as in its home country, Germany.

SPECIFIC INFORMATION DIFFUSION NETWORKS FOR TELECOMMUNICATIONS

More than most people probably realize, telecommunications systems in any particular country are strongly affected by institutions beyond national borders. Three in particular form the basis of this part of my study: the ITU, the WB, and the OECD. Although other information networks exist, these three are particularly important in the spread of ideas and policies for telecommunications regulatory reform.

The International Telecommunications Union

The ITU is one of the first international organizations, existing for 145 years with 191 member countries and more than 700 sector members and associates. As part of the United Nations (UN) system, headquartered in Geneva, the ITU uses a one-nation, one-vote system to coordinate shared radio spectrum, satellite orbits, and telecommunications development. The ITU can be seen as an information network for three reasons: (1) it plays a key role in creating and disseminating research reports, surveys, and websites concerned with telecom regulatory reform; (2) it provides multiple forums of conferences and meetings in which actors can meet and interact; and (3) there is no sanctioning power for membership, nor is there a strict enforcement mechanism for harmonization. The ITU issues yearly publications of data on telecommunications markets and regulation, reports on international telecommunications developments around the world, and studies of the global information society. Some examples include the publication of World Telecommunications Indicators, the Global Regulatory Database, and *Trends in Telecommunications*.[1] The ITU also convenes conferences on best practices in regulation that are organized through the bureau of development, the regulatory department, and the office for strategy and planning.

The ITU traditionally has been the forum for states to get together and agree on technical standards and developing goals. Although the ITU used to be more of a cartel – a cozy monopoly between state-owned monopolists – its role has been changing over the past years. The ITU remains affiliated with the United Nations, is centered in Geneva, and has a voting structure of one-nation, one-vote.

Currently, the ITU is most active in promoting regulatory reform in telecommunications through its department for development and regulation (ITU-D). The ITU facilitates a dialogue between regulators on a regional as well global level, and holds annual meetings in which regulators meet and discuss common challenges for effective regulation, from the development of new pricing schemes to agreeing on the definitions of significant market power (SMP), new policies for universal access, and interconnection pricing regimes. Furthermore, in recent conferences, such as the World Dialogue on Regulation (WDR) and the World Summit on the Information Society (WSIS), some of these actors are representatives of ministries, new independent regulators, and even private sector actors. More information on the WSIS can be found at the websites for the World Dialogue on Regulation (http://www.regulateonline.org/) and the World Summit on the Information Society (http://www.itu.int/wsis/index.html).

[1] http://www.itu.int/publications

Still active in terms of providing forums for the spread of information and best practices, training for regulators, training for policy-makers, and the like, the ITU provides a yearly survey of telecommunications and information communications sectors, and also hosts a website for the Global Regulators Exchange (G-REX). This website, launched by the Telecommunications Development Bureau of the ITU (BDT) in 2011, offers a forum for the exchange of information, views, and experiences of regulatory issues. According to the ITU-BDT website, "regulatory information is key to creating an enabling environment to bridge the digital divide" (www.itu.int/ITU-D/grex).

Although the ITU definitely provides a forum in which experts and member states can gather and exchange information and best practices about the regulation of telecommunications and the information society, it does not have much "teeth" in terms of requiring countries to take action for regulatory reform. Also, much of the action in establishing separate regulatory institutions happened after telecommunications policy was reframed as a trade issue, particularly that of trade in services, and has thus shifted over to the WTO. As we will see later, the role of the WTO in creating and promoting similar institutional innovations in telecommunications was critical in the spread of liberal, market-oriented reforms around the world.

The World Bank

One does not often think of the WB when thinking about telecom, yet reforming that sector is in line with the Bank's established goal for promoting economic development worldwide. In this regard, the Bank's role is more in information gathering and facilitation, and far less in coercion, as has been suggested in other studies. Some of the key activities of the WB in telecommunications are in research, as well as in the creation of InfoDEV, a financing organization.[2] One of the larger umbrella organizations for telecommunications regulatory reform is the World Dialogue on Regulation (WDR), which is

[2] http://www.infodev.org

housed in the WB.[3] The WB handbook on telecom regulation was an instrument for the diffusion of best practices, as well as for the diffusion of basic principles and techniques of telecom regulation and policy (Intven, Oliver, and Sepulveda 2000). This handbook stressed the importance of competition and of establishing separate regulatory institutions, but not necessarily privatization.

One way in which the WB research unit affected some policy changes was through research symposia (Wellenius 1989, 1993), the publication of *Public Policy for the Private Sector* leaflets, and its recommendations on telecommunications reform. In the early phases, the Bank focused primarily on the privatization of telecom incumbents; in later phases, the Bank turned its focus to introducing competition and other forms of regulatory reform (Wellenius and Staple 1996; Wellenius and Stern 1994). Most of the WB's earlier work on telecom regulatory reform focused on liberalization (lifting entry requirements, licenses, and quotas) and also on privatization of the telecom incumbent. The early WB articles did not focus on the need to have a separate and independent telecom regulator, although that emphasis increased over time (Wallsten 2002). For example, in the early works on the Telecommunications Policy for the Private Sector, part of the Bank's Private Sector Development efforts, the Bank emphasized many of the perceived benefits of telecom reform.

In addition to producing information and research on regulatory reform in telecommunications, the WB has provided material support and incentives for telecom restructuring. The Bank has provided financing through loans for the expansion of telecommunications infrastructure in the past, usually through the state-owned postal, telegraph, and telephone services (PTTs). The WB shifted its policy since the mid-1990s, when lending to state-owned enterprises became contingent on sector reform, including an exit strategy for government ownership and operation of telecom operators (Intven et al. 2000).

The WB became more active in the promotion of ideas and best practices in telecommunications when it partnered with the ITU

[3] http://www.wdr.org

on its ICT-Eye regulatory database. In 2006, the WB published a handbook for evaluating infrastructure regulatory systems, and stated that the independent regulatory agencies model is the de facto standard worldwide for sectorwide regulation (Brown, Stern et al. 2006).

The WB continues to issue policy papers and projects on information and communications technology and development, yet countries have a wide variation in when and how they implement these suggested reforms.

Organization for Economic Cooperation and Development

The Organization for Economic Cooperation and Development (OECD) is another source of information and policy cues on regulatory reforms. Founded in 1961 and headquartered in Paris, France, the OECD now has thirty-four members committed to democracy and a market economy, with another group of countries participating in dialogue with the OECD for possible accession "enlargement" (including Russia) or "enhanced engagement" (with Brazil, China, India, Indonesia, South Africa).[4]

According to its mission statement, "The Organization provides a setting where governments compare policy experiences, seek answers to common problems, identify good practice and coordinate domestic and international policies" (OECD Mission Statement, available at http://www.oecd.org/about/). The OECD does not deploy mechanisms of coercion or enforcement for the adoption of market-oriented policies on its members. It does, however, include instruments of Recommendations and Decisions as part of membership in the OECD, and it sends experts to work with countries on specific topics. It also issues country studies of various market sectors. The field of regulatory reform is one of its key fields, for both new as well as older members. The OECD Regulatory Reform unit (as well as its Competition unit) has conducted and published many studies of countries and their progress in telecommunications reform. In 2001, the OECD made a Recommendation

[4] http://www.oecd.org

of the Council of Ministers (C2001)78, concerning the structural separation of regulated industry.[5]

In many ways, the OECD can be viewed as a source of ideational pressure, through the interaction of policy experts and other countries. There do not seem to be material incentives that benefit the OECD directly – although the goals of regulatory reform in telecommunications are couched in terms of increasing material benefit for all. In this way, the ideals behind the OECD are based in liberal market ideology, and are carried by economists and other policy experts. The OECD can be viewed as a kind of epistemic community for liberal economic reform, based on the principle of free trade, free markets, and competition.

Regulation of telecommunications takes place within a larger context of reform more generally, and the calculus of government decision-makers often rests on the overall climate for liberal economic reform. Despite its image as a kind of club of wealthy and prosperous countries, the OECD is part of a larger epistemic community and policy network for regulatory reform in telecommunications, which is different from other international organizations in that it has very little coercive power, with not much of a disciplining mechanism. Yet, the ideational premise, as mentioned earlier, is rooted in a commitment to liberal market ideology, and thus it carries a coherent message in terms of how countries are committed to reform, and it signals to investors about their commitment to reform. After a ministerial meeting in 1996, the OECD began to conduct in-depth country studies on "regulatory reform" that were subsequently peer-reviewed by all member states. These were then published under a series on regulatory reform in telecommunications (OECD 1997, 2000b, 2000c), as well as in other sectors, including trucking, shipping, air transport, electricity, and financial services – sectors that traditionally have been closed, one-country models.

This peer-review process can be understood as a process of information sharing, as well as of peer pressure among policy

[5] http://www.oecd.org/document/31/0,3746,en_2649_34753_44942431_1_1_1_1,00.html

experts, other member states, and other regulators. As will be shown in Chapter 4, for the Czech Republic, these studies began in cooperation with an office within the Ministry of the Interior that was tasked with studying the conditions of regulation across a wide range of sectors. Eventually, this office was moved into the Government Office and given authority to draft new legislation on the establishment of an act on the establishment of new regulatory authorities for various sectors. Many of these recommendations emerged from the process of interaction with other experts through the context of the OECD peer review.[6]

The OECD established a section on the study of regulatory reform in 1997, and, since then, has issued several research papers and reports on the goals of regulation and various measures for effectiveness across a wide range of sectors, including railroads, airlines, telecommunications (Boylaud and Nicoletti 2000), electricity (Steiner 2000), and other areas that were prime foci of deregulation movements. In addition to publishing research reports, the OECD sponsored a Regulatory Database, gathered by Boylaud and Nicoletti. The goal was to compare and contrast the regulatory reform efforts of members of the OECD, of which telecommunications was one sector (OECD 2002). Some of these papers attempted to develop concepts and measures for regulatory intervention, with varying success (Nicoletti and Pryor 2001).

The OECD conducted many peer-reviewed studies of regulatory reform in various sectors. Some of the countries in this book that actively engaged the OECD peer review process included the Czech Republic (OECD 2001), Denmark (OECD 2000a), Finland (OECD 2003), Hungary (OECD 2000b), the Netherlands (OECD 1999), and Poland (OECD 2002a), among others.[7] The OECD sent teams of researchers and experts to various member countries – both new and old members – to study the state of the art in regulation and what the countries were doing. The process of engaging in this self-study and peer review led many countries,

[6] Interview with Czech policy-makers, 2003.

[7] These reports are publicly available at http://www.oecd.org.

including some profiled in this book, to change their regulatory reform policies, at least in telecommunications. For example, in the Czech Republic, the regulatory reform unit was moved from the Ministry of Interior into the Department of Government.

Committing to OECD membership and to peer review was an important step for many of the countries under study, signaling their commitment to market liberalism in trade, competition, and other areas of reform. I argue that this commitment to market liberalism, as shown through networks affiliated with international market trade, facilitated the channels through which principles of regulatory reform were able to flow. This demonstrates that commitment to a liberal market is even more important than is an actual market force. Governments play a role in signaling to investors and trading partners that the state is committed to opening markets to competition and investment, which is a kind of constructivist approach, yet one that follows along market principles, not those of global identities.

This ideological consensus was held by economists, researchers, and technocrats and – in an atmosphere of uncertainty, as well as of the promise of great gains and rewards – it was spread by government decision-makers. Yet, the liberal consensus is not value-neutral, as can be seen in the arena of global finance in 2008 and beyond. Other studies emanating from the OECD include the annual publication of its Communications Outlook, country economic surveys, and studies of information and communications technology adoption in the Digital Age.

Diffusion through information networks is one of the three channels of reform, and the mechanisms for such diffusion resemble mimesis and learning. The next channel of reform, diffusion through harmonization networks, has more of an element of coercion and competition.

DIFFUSION THROUGH HARMONIZATION NETWORKS IN TELECOMMUNICATIONS

Many accounts present hypotheses of international organizations (the WTO, the EU) and "big states" (the United States, France) as coercive agents, forcing their interests and regulations on hapless followers (Drezner 2005). Yet, simple theories of coercion overlook the subtler power dynamics involved in these policy processes, as well as in the opportunities for the "recipient" countries to vary substantially in their implementation of the received wisdom. My analysis draws upon Nye's distinction between hard and soft power. *Hard power* is the "command power that can be used to induce others to change their position" (Nye 2002).

According to this logic, telecom decision-makers in various countries enact policy change and establish new separate telecom authorities because the WTO, WB, or EU force them to change their status quo position, either through incentives or sanctions, through carrots or sticks.

This does not, however, explain the observed outcomes. For example, although EU regulations mandate that all countries must have a regulatory authority separate from the incumbent, there is no requirement that countries establish a new separate regulatory agency. I argue that the concept of "soft power" has more leverage. *Soft power* has more to do with persuasion and agenda-setting, the ability to persuade others that they want what you want. Although power is involved in these relations, it is not direct coercion but something more like persuasion. The mechanism is much closer to that of emulation, learning, and mimicry, notwithstanding the power relations involved.

The first key exemplar of harmonization networks is the World Trade Organization (WTO), through its membership in general, through country commitments to the Basic Agreement on Telecommunications Services under the General Agreement on Trade in Services (GATS), and through the Reference Paper for Telecommunications, all of which fall under the authority of the WTO dispute settlement mechanism (DSM). The second exemplar in this study is the European Union (EU). In the EU, harmonization occurs in regard to conditions for overall membership in the EU and adoption of the *acquis communautaire*, but also to the particularities of the New Regulatory Framework for electronic commerce and associated directives and institutional requirements. These aspects are subject to the authority of the

European Court of Justice (ECJ). These networks are explored in further detail later.

World Trade Organization

The WTO, as shown later, became more institutionalized in 1995, right around the time of the technological shift in telecommunications, as well as with an ideological shift toward more liberal market principles. Telecommunications was reframed in a new way – it became a trade issue. There was a shift in the telecom industry from one of international regulation and the cozy monopoly of states and engineers to a free-trade issue concerned with market access and liberal market economy. This symbolized a commitment to open markets – to efforts to introduce some degree of competition, or at least to provide the opportunity to make money. Big countries wanted to do this – but then smaller countries signed on. The logic of liberal trade in services represented a kind of reconceptualization of interdependence and globalization, which had implications for international organizations and markets. When telecommunications became a tradeable cross-border investment, it became a different kind of animal altogether. Powerful economic countries, especially the United States, led the movement to shift the governance of telecommunications from the cozy monopoly system of the ITU to the liberal, market-oriented focus of the WTO.

One of the first organizations to promote free trade was the General Agreement on Tariffs and Trade (GATT), founded in 1948 by thirty-two "contracting parties." There were eight rounds of the GATT before it was subsumed under the formation of the WTO in 1995. By 2002, there were 158 trading partners covered by 144 members of the WTO. In addition, a number of "observers" committed to begin negotiations with the WTO within five years. These observers include Algeria, Andorra, Russia, and Saudi Arabia. Not all countries in the world are members or observers of the WTO, and some countries that do not participate at all include Afghanistan, Iraq, Liberia, and Syria. Yet, this also indicates that most countries around the world, including China, have become members of this organization, which promotes the principles and practices of free trade (Krueger and Aturupane 1998).

One of the features of the WTO includes the dispute-settlement mechanism (DSM), which can make and enforce binding decisions in the case of violations of free-trade agreements, a difference from the GATT system (Cameron and Campbell 1998; Reinhart 2001). Therefore, countries that commit to membership in the overall organization and to the specific schedules of commitments to the treaty could be subject to penalty in case of violation. Put another way, countries can demonstrate their commitment to the principles of free trade by signing this binding commitment.

Within telecommunications, which is covered under the General Agreement on Trade in Services (GATS) Annex on Telecommunications Services, one of the principal instruments is the 1996 WTO Agreement on Basic Telecommunications, put into effect in 1997. Some observers argue that the WTO Agreement on Basic Telecommunications "fundamentally changed expectations and norms about the operation of the international market that will in turn change the economic options of even the countries that made no WTO commitments" (Cowhey and Klimenko 2001).

More than seventy-nine governments signed the 1997 WTO Basic Agreement and made commitments to the Reference Paper. The process of negotiating the Basic Agreement and the promise of great expected economic gains and foreign investment helped the organization promote and shape preferences for reform, namely that of establishing a separate regulatory agency. In addition, it became a forum for expert discussion, as those familiar with telecommunications and services negotiated each country's schedule of commitments to the Basic Agreement and the Reference Paper, and learned from the other negotiators at the table about best practices (Singh 2008).

Some of the criteria listed in the Reference Paper, which became binding commitments under the GATS and subject to the authority of the Dispute Settlement Understanding, included the liberalization of market segments and the establishment of separate regulatory authorities for telecommunications. We might expect countries to establish new regulatory authorities for telecom and to liberalize market segments in response to these conditions of the Reference Paper. Yet, in the econometric analysis, signing the WTO Basic Agreement on Telecommunications had no significant statistical relationship with the timing of regulatory reform. Upon closer study, it becomes clear that many states had already begun to make market-opening reforms prior to signing the WTO Agreement.

For the WTO, it makes sense that countries would anticipate the Basic Agreement on Telecommunications, especially as some of the terms of the Reference Paper began to be discussed under the GATS well prior to the reforms in the early 1990s. The Reference Paper, like the EU directives, did not specify the importance of privatizing the telecom incumbent or introducing private sector participation into the sector. The Reference Paper did, however, emphasize the importance of liberal market access and also the importance of having a regulator separate from the dominant incumbent operator. Although this does not meet the criteria for an independent regulator according to the ITU, this is a step toward a more separate regulatory authority. Others have written extensively about the negotiating process and its effects, including some calls for the strengthening of WTO requirements in the telecoms area (Singh 2002, 2008). The Basic Agreement was definitely an achievement, spearheaded by the United States but also joined by developing countries.

Yet, despite the promise of the WTO and its possible coercive mechanism through the dispute settlement system, it appears that the real power lies elsewhere. For example, although more than seventy-nine countries signed the Basic Agreement on Telecommunications and although it is certainly a part of the GATS, there is not a big bureaucracy at the WTO devoted to telecommunications issues. There is one person who is the main telecom expert, along with a team of other experts who are consulted on a case-by-case basis, and there is a list of possible judges for the DSM in regards to telecom issues. The WTO building in Geneva is quite large, yet the representation of telecoms is quite small, at least in terms of numbers. Also, the process of using the DSM is member-driven, as seen in the one important case on telecommunications reviewed under the DSM – the case of the *United States* v *Mexico*, in which the WTO ruled that Mexico was indeed in violation of its WTO commitments for open market access and interconnection, and Mexico subsequently passed legislation in 2005 to reflect these changes (Wilson 2007).

The Basic Agreement, along with other provisions of the GATS, was scheduled to be renegotiated entirely under the Doha Round, and it does not appear that there will be a new multilateral agreement on basic telecommunications.

The European Union

The process of regulatory reform within the growing European Union (EU) has reflected the broader process of economic and political integration. As the overall EU moves toward a single market, the goals in the telecommunications and information services sector have been to create a single market for telecommunications services and equipment. The tools for achieving a single market in services have ranged from progressive liberalization of former monopoly operators and harmonization of regulations and standards, to the introduction of competition rules. Yet, although the EU directives required member states to lift restrictions on ownership and special privileges for public enterprises, they did not specify the privatization of firms or services. The norm was for liberalization and re-regulation (by introducing and enforcing competition), but not for privatization.

Majone describes how privatization was never part of the European integration project. The Treaty of Rome showed great comfort with state intervention in the economy, particularly in France, Italy, and Germany, which all have large public sectors. There was no ideology of privatization at the level of the EU. Yet, there was an ideology of competition and for elements of liberal reform. If countries were to create a market out of heavily regulated national markets, they would need to introduce competition and shift regulation. Some of the tools of EU integration included liberalization (lifting restrictions on the single market), harmonization (ensuring minimal standards, mutual recipes, and essential equivalence of regulations), and competition (Majone 1996).

Some of the justification for harmonization was that it would reduce transaction costs and increase the benefits for businesses and consumers, and that it would reduce the costs of services. Furthermore, although the norm for liberalization in the late 1990s and early 2000s spread, and the functional form of the national regulatory agencies began to take hold, the results were not complete harmonization of regulation. After ten years, the European Commission wrote that

> [W]hilst the current EU regulatory framework has brought benefits to European citizens in terms of innovative and increasingly affordable electronic communications services some serious obstacles still need to be overcome. There are still concerns regarding the independence and the effectiveness of national regulatory authorities ... consumers and businesses are still faced with 27 different markets and thus are not able to take advantage of the economic potential of a single market.
>
> (European Commission 2009)

The EU can be understood as a powerful international actor that drives reform in several ways. One of the most direct ways in which the EU has taken action is through promoting the 1987 Green Paper on Telecommunications Reform, the 1990 White Paper, and the subsequent directives on electronic commerce in 2002 and 2009. Both member states and new accession members must "harmonize" domestic legislation to that of the common market. The EU drives changes not only in its member states and those poised to accede, but it also acts in the international arenas of the WTO, the ITU, and directly with the United States and Japan. Furthermore, developments in the EU provide a focal point for other countries seeking to enact telecom regulatory reform, particularly those countries that are parliamentary systems, former European colonies, or that trade heavily with the EU. The process of EU enlargement increases the frequency and nature of interaction among policy-makers and policy elites and can generate policy learning as policy-makers "get the facts right" and acquire "common knowledge" (Risse 2000).

I show later how the EU fulfilled the role of a harmonization network by promoting and shaping preferences for the regulation of the telecommunications/electronic communications markets and acting as a forum for the exchange of expert opinions and the exchange of best practices.

A simple explanation for liberal regulatory reform in telecommunications is that the countries were forced to implement these reforms due to their overall commitment to join the EU. If they sought to be part of the common market, they needed to adopt the same directives and parallel legislation as EU member states, in the telecom sector as well as other aspects of the *acquis communautaire*.

A possible mechanism for this liberal policy adoption in the simple scenario is coercion, in which members or accession countries have little choice about how and when to adopt the *acquis* on telecommunications regulation. There might be a time lag in the adoption of policy reform, but all states eventually would have to implement the *acquis* in order to be admitted as members in May 2004, or to avoid punishment through the European Court of Justice (ECJ). Yet, a simple correlation between accession to the EU and adoption of liberal policy reform, explained by a mechanism of coercion, seems a bit too simplistic and cannot explain the more complicated and interdependent ties between the Commission, various member states, and emerging governance mechanisms for regulatory cooperation.

The EU also has special instruments for its relationships with member states of Central and Eastern Europe (CEE). The Program of Community Aid to the Countries of Central and Eastern Europe (PHARE) is one of three preaccession instruments designed to assist applicant countries of central Europe in their preparations for joining the EU. PHARE's preaccession focus was put into place especially after 1997, in response to the Luxembourg Council's launching of the accession projects. One of the key programs included "twinning," in which sector members, particularly regulators, were paired with regulators in EU member states in order to draft programs of regulatory reform and policies.[8] These ranged

[8] http://europa.eu.int/comm/enlargement/pas/twinning/index.html

from short-term expert visits (STE) to longer-term secondment of experts to the regulatory agencies of the accession countries, with the expenses paid through the PHARE twinning office.

I argue that although the EU played a critical role in the adoption and implementation of standards, the mechanism was much more than simple coercion, in which decisions taken elsewhere are simply translated and implemented into domestic legislation. I argue that the EU provided material incentives, but also acted as a source of policy cues and information about best practices for new member states. Furthermore, although some argue that the EU has become more decentralized, its efforts in Eastern Europe reflect more a hub-and-spokes relationship between accession countries and the Commission, rather than spoke-spoke cooperation and collaboration among Eastern European countries themselves. Furthermore, over time, the EU's efforts have become even more critical in the development and implementation of pro-competition re-regulation, as well as in the strengthening of regulators, particularly through the development of two bodies of governance – the Independent Regulators Group (IRG) and the European Regulators Group (ERG) – and its subsequent establishment of the Body of European Regulators of Electronic Communications (BEREC) in 2009.

European Framework for the Information Society

The EU regulatory framework seeks to ensure that all citizens, no matter where they live, have access to basic telecommunications services, including voice and internet, at a reasonable and affordable price. Competition among operators has been deemed one form of ensuring lower prices for consumers. Yet, in many market segments, incumbent operators, mostly monopolies, continue to dominate the sector, and regulators must ensure that they do not use their position unfairly to squeeze out competitors.

The current regulatory framework in the EU is based on a package of five Directives and a Regulation:

- Directive (2002/21/EC) on a common regulatory framework, as amended by Directive 2009/140/EC ("Better Regulation Directive")

- Directive (2002/19/EC) on access and interconnection as amended by Directive 2009/140/EC ("Better Regulation Directive")
- Directive (2002/20/EC) on the authorization of electronic communications networks and services as amended by Directive 2009/140/EC ("Better Regulation Directive")
- Directive (2002/22/EC) on universal service and users' rights relating to electronic communications networks and services as amended by 2009/136/EC Directive ("Citizen' Rights Directive")
- Directive (2002/58/EC) on privacy and electronic communications as amended by Directive 2009/136/EC ("Citizens' Rights Directive")
- Regulation (EC) No 1211/2009 of the European Parliament and of the Council of November 25, 2009, establishing the Body of European Regulators for Electronic Communications (BEREC) and the Office.

NETWORKS OF REGULATORS WITHIN TELECOMMUNICATIONS

Networks of new telecom agencies have emerged on the international level, with the World Dialogue on Regulation and an international regulators conference that meets under the auspices of the ITU every year. This regulator network has working groups on key issues of institutions and policies. In addition to global networks of regulators, each region has one or more networks of regulators.

Historically, there were two main regulator networks in Europe, the Independent Regulators Group (IRG) and the European Regulators Group (ERG). The former was an older, looser, more informal group of regulators that exchanged information and best practices on institutions and policies. The latter was more formalized and became part of the governance structure of the EU. This association of national regulatory authorities provided information and recommendations to the European Commission, particularly the Director General for Information Society and Competition.

This newer network of regulators actually had teeth, and its decision-making procedures reinforced the need for the IRG to develop more of a consensus.

The IRG[9] was founded in 1997 and consisted of regulators from the EU, the European Free Trade Area (EFTA), and the European Economic Area. The chairmen of the affiliated regulators met four times a year, and members exchanged information and experience throughout the year in meetings, seminars, and working groups. The IRG issued compilations of these experiences in its Principles of Implementation and Best Practices (PIBS). Some of these PIBs included discussions of local loop unbundling (LLU), cooperation with competition authorities, and separation of financial reporting. The members of the IRG also include those countries of the new Europe-25, including those profiled in Chapter 4. The IRG has overlapping membership with the ERG (listed below); the IRG provides a forum for information exchange and best practices, whereas the ERG has more authority from the EU. These differences are similar to those of the two types of diffusion networks (diffusion networks of information vs. diffusion networks of harmonization). In the IRG, horizontal relations are obtained among regulators and across government lines, whereas in a more typical diffusion network, it is international organizations that mediate diffusion.

The ERG was created by Commission Decision 2002/627/EC, adopted on July 29, 2002. The ERG was an independent body for reflection, debate, and advice in the electronic communications regulatory field. Composed of the heads of the relevant national authorities, it acted as an interface between them and the European Commission in order to advise and assist the Commission in consolidating the internal market for electronic communications networks and services.

The ERG provided a forum and a network for regulators to tap into expertise and allies when pressured politically and institutionally in the domestic markets. With the ERG, some hoped that the uniform interpretation of the EU directives in telecommunications

[9] For more current information, please consult http://www.irg.int.

could be promoted by soft steering of expert goals, through frequent interactions with other regulators, and through the policy transfer of best practices in telecom regulation (Majone 2000).

The ERG provided pressure on both national regulatory authorities and political actors through institutional isomorphism and through a process of active monitoring and benchmarking of national practice. Coen argued that these networks can influence the development of a national regime through naming and shaming of governments that are too interventionist or regulators that have been captured by business. He also maintained that these networks help improve the flows of information and personnel to create a more stable regulatory regime (Coen and Heritier 2005).

HARMONIZATION AND REGULATORY NETWORKS: THE ROLE OF THE EUROPEAN COMMISSION

The European Commission has the power, through Article 7 and 7a of the Framework Directive for Electronic Communications, to oversee draft national regulatory approaches through consultation at the EU level, which is designed to consolidate and strengthen the internal market. Member state national regulator agencies (NRAs) are required to provide analyses of those telecom products and services markets that may require ex ante regulation and impose obligations. NRAs use the Commission's "Recommendation" on relevant markets as a starting point, as well as its Guidelines on market analysis and assessment of significant market power (SMP). If an NRA concludes that a given market is not competitive, it must impose a regulatory obligation in line with universal service and market access. European Union consultations are known as "Article 7 procedures" and seek to ensure cooperation among NRAs, and between the NRAs and the Commission.

This is an example of diffusion through both harmonization networks and regulator networks, particularly as the EU institutionalized the relationship among NRAs through the regulatory frameworks themselves, the EU Consultation procedures (Article 7), and the creation of the BEREC.

The BEREC and the Office (based in Latvia) were created to improve consistency of the EU regulatory framework. The BEREC replaces the ERG, through which NRAs exchanged expertise and best practice and gave opinions on the functioning of the telecom market in the EU. The BEREC moves a step further and gives advice to EU institutions and works, "to complement at European level the regulatory tasks performed at national level by the regulatory authorities" (BEREC 2012). The BEREC's main tasks are to participate in single-market consultations (Article 7); give opinions on cross-border disputes; disseminate best practices; advise the Commission, Parliament, and Council; assist the NRAs; and deliver opinions. This group provides a platform for regulators to coordinate cross-border policies, create and share best practices, study new market developments, and advise the European Commission and other EU bodies. The Board is composed of the heads of the twenty-seven national telecommunications regulators and is assisted by an Office. Decisions are made by majority rule of the twenty-seven national NRAs.

SPREAD OF REFORMS FROM INTERNATIONAL AGENCIES TO DOMESTIC INNOVATIONS

Ideas, Norms, Mimesis, and Learning

This book is very sympathetic to the approach of constructivists and scholars who treat ideas and norms seriously, although the focus here is more on institutions and policy outcomes. As some have written, ideas do not flow freely (Risse-Kappen 1994), but rather are carried by actors within systems (Yee 1996). Some of the studies in political science include the role of social learning in European integration (Haas 1964), economic policy (Jacobsen 1995), the study of epistemic communities (Haas 1992), how ideas affect European politics (McNamara 1998), how ideas affect cooperation between North and South (Sell 1998), how ideas affect the structure and policies of corporate governance (Ziegler 1997), how ideas affect neoliberal policies (Biersteker 1995; Blyth 1997), and which ideas spread in area of Asian regionalism (Acharya 2004). In this book, I assume neoliberal policy ideas as a constant global force and a source of common pressure for change, underlying many policy advocates and embedded within international institutions, especially in the international organizations I study.

Others analyze institutional isomorphism and focus on imitation and mimesis as a mechanism, and some recent scholars have studied the spread of liberal reforms through the lens of emulation and learning (Brinks and Coppedge 2006; Henisz, Zelner, and Guillen 2004; Lee and Strang 2006; Padgett 2003). Governments learn about the effects of enacting telecom reforms by observing the experiments of other governments. These foreign lessons are then incorporated into national telecom regulatory reform. Governments face uncertainty over how to regulate a dynamic, capital-intensive, knowledge economy. Most governments have little experience in regulating *for* competition, as the dominant paradigm for telecom regulation was government-owned and -operated telecom monopolies. Thus, it is unlikely that a government would be able to draw conclusions over the most efficient or most appropriate way to regulate a dynamic and competitive market on the basis of its experience alone. I argue that there is substantial opportunity for both mimesis and learning and the creation and adoption of regulatory reform in telecommunications. Even markets in advanced countries are characterized by asymmetric information in the regulation and governance of telecommunications, and it is clear that most countries face challenges in their regulatory capacity to identify risk and mitigate conflicts of interest.

COUNTRY-LEVEL SOURCES OF TRENDS AND VARIATION IN TELECOM REFORM

Although I argue that international organizations provide an important forum and source for liberal telecom reform that has been understudied in much of the literature on reform, there are also many important sources of trend and variation within countries. Some of these actors and mechanisms were mentioned in Chapter 1 and are well-treated in much of the literature on political economy. For example, interest groups are often an important source of pressure and constraints on government regulatory reform, particularly in telecommunications. As mentioned in Chapter 1, all countries have entrenched interests in the main telecom operator, which can either accelerate or impede some aspects of telecom reform. Government policy-makers around the world struggle to balance the roles of making policy, creating regulation, and establishing conditions for new alternative operators with ensuring future benefits for consumers. Some states will be more or less successful in designing regulatory institutions, particularly "effective" regulators. Two determining factors include government's political leadership and commitment to reform, and also a government's capacity for reform. We would expect countries to vary along these two key dimensions.

Furthermore, as stressed in the political economy literature, other political and economic configurations of countries can be pivotal in explaining government preferences, strategies, and outcomes of telecommunications reform. Although my analysis focuses more on questions of timing and how countries respond to triggers of reform over the past twenty years, it is also necessary to include some of the political structures through which countries can respond to these reform triggers. The San Diego School often focuses on whether countries are parliamentary or presidential systems, their degree of federalism, and the extent of checks and balances in a system (Cox and McCubbins 2001). I test whether some of these specific hypotheses seem to be at play in the econometric analysis, although the cases selected are all democratic parliamentary systems, so that factor in particular cannot be explored at length in the case studies.

SPECIFIC HYPOTHESES

Building on this framework of international actors and mechanisms, it is possible to outline the following specific hypotheses. It is likely that membership in liberal international organizations will increase the likelihood that countries will adopt liberal telecoms reforms. The more important international organization hypotheses for this book are the specific roles of the OECD, the WTO, and the EU.

Hypothesis 1: Organization for Economic Cooperation and Development

We would expect countries that are members of the OECD to be more likely to adopt the principles of liberal telecom reform, particularly those of liberalization, re-regulation, and the establishment of separate regulatory bodies. Countries also would be more likely to establish these regulators around the time of actual OECD studies of telecom regulatory reform, particularly in the peer-review process. Membership in the OECD can be analyzed in the econometric analysis, and a country's specific relationship with the OECD can be demonstrated in the case analysis. The posited mechanism would be that of information-generation and transmission, solidified by the peer-reviewed process of the OECD reports.

Hypothesis 2: World Trade Organization

Countries that are members of the WTO are more likely to adopt liberal telecom reforms, particularly after the time period of the Basic Agreement on Telecommunications Services. Although countries that join the WTO may be more prone to liberalize some sectors of the economy in terms of trade, this does not necessarily translate into more microeconomic and sectoral considerations. Membership in the WTO could indicate a willingness of countries to commit to general principles of market access for trade. Membership in the WTO also indicates that countries have a forum in which they are exposed to the practices of other countries, either through the schedule of commitments or actual policy behavior.

One hypothesis is that membership in the WTO would increase a country's likelihood of enacting liberal telecom reform, particularly in the areas of liberalization and establishing a separate regulatory authority. The WTO does not place limitations on state ownership, however, and remains agnostic about the necessity for privatization, as long as a market is open to access and provides national treatment to foreign companies in various market segments. Therefore, we would not expect membership in the WTO to be associated with the timing of privatization of the telecom incumbent.

Another hypothesis relates to the actual commitment to the WTO Basic Agreement in Telecommunications Services. We might expect countries that commit to the WTO Basic Agreement to be more likely to enact liberal reform in the areas of market access and establishment of separate regulators. These hypotheses can be tested both in the econometric analysis and in the case studies by analyzing each country's schedule of commitments to the Basic Agreement on Telecommunications Service and whether those countries adopt the Reference Paper, a set of guidelines on market opening principles.

Hypothesis 3: European Union

Countries that are members of the EU or are planning to join the EU will be more likely to adhere to its telecom directives and regulations. Under the 1998 package, countries were supposed to establish regulators separate from the dominant incumbent, and we would expect to observe these new separate regulators emerging around that time (or a bit later in the case of accession countries). The EU does not, however, stipulate conditions for privatization, so membership will most likely not be related to privatization outcomes. Countries can vary in their relationship with the EU, however, both with the Commission and the Directives, as well as under the PHARE project for accession countries. (Some of these trends and variations are explored in particular case studies.) Since Europe is one of the most important regions in terms of pioneering liberal telecom reforms in the 1990s, I chose this region to study countries in more depth. Unfortunately, in the global economic analysis, membership in the EU is collinear with the region of Western Europe, so it was only possible to test regional hypotheses and not the independent effect of EU membership. Yet, this is explored in much more depth and detail in the case analysis.

Hypothesis 4: Regulatory Networks

Most countries began to liberalize their economies in the 1990s, prior to the establishment of the regulatory networks. Thus, when asking questions about the timing of reform, it does not make sense to ask about the role of regulatory networks. Yet, these networks are crucial in the enactment of regulatory reform, especially in the design of particular regulatory processes. For example, we would expect countries that are members of the ERG to be more likely to adopt its general principles on universal service obligations, the regulation of interconnection agreements with incumbents across technological platforms, and specific details of pricing mechanism (long-run average incremental costs, etc.). Some of these can be observed in the case studies, although it is more likely that the role of these regulatory networks is just beginning to emerge.

ALTERNATIVE EXPLANATIONS 1: OTHER INTERNATIONAL ORGANIZATIONS

Although all countries are members of the ITU, we might expect its influence on countries to vary by income and level of development. For example, it is possible that poor countries that participate in the regulatory workshops held by the ITU-D organization will be more likely to enact liberal reform at a later time than will richer countries, especially after benefiting not only from prior examples of other members but also from the expertise of the actual regulatory workshops and sessions within the ITU. Rich countries might be more likely to reform more quickly if they are competitive, or less quickly if they can afford not to change. The prediction for middle-income countries, especially as relative to the ITU, is ambiguous.

The WB may or may not have an independent effect on the timing of liberal telecom reform adoption, and, as with the ITU, it would be more likely to affect developing countries and at a later time. One of the channels of influence that would affect the timing of reform is the issuance of country studies, expert visits, and also the granting of WB financial support for telecommunications project. We might expect that if the WB granted support for a particular telecommunications project, that country would be more likely to liberalize its telecom sector either after beginning the project or perhaps a short time before the project begins, in anticipation of funding. This hypothesis is tested in the data in the econometric analysis. Yet, the case studies for this book do not reveal much variation in WB involvement, as the countries under study do not have much WB activity.

ALTERNATIVE EXPLANATIONS 2: INTERNATIONAL MARKETS

One explanation for the timing of reform is that of U.S. power and international markets, as shown through the international accounting rate paid to foreign carriers over time (FCC 2004). In 1997, the U.S. unilaterally changed the procedures for the international settlement rate (Cave and Waverman 1998; Wallsten 2001).

The settlement rate (and thus revenues) dropped over time, and we might expect that this drop in revenues might increase the pressure on governments to enact domestic regulatory reform because they could no longer rely on the cash-cow of international settlement payments to finance their domestic telecom markets and infrastructure needs. Conversely, a higher international accounting rate could also increase the rate of reform adoption. One possibility is that countries with high international settlement rates might be in more need of eventual reform, as most of the highest rates were for developing countries in distant markets, as opposed to more competitive routes (e.g., United States to London). Therefore, these countries would be encouraged to reform sooner, given that revenues eventually would shift to market levels and also because existing infrastructure might be particularly in need of reform. This hypothesis can be tested in both the econometric analysis and the case studies.

A second international economy explanation is the level of foreign debt held by countries. Countries with high debt services in relation to exports (and thus more dependent on trade to raise revenues) may be more likely to privatize the incumbent to raise revenues and to send a signal to private investors about a government's credible commitment to a competitive market environment. It is possible to test this hypothesis in both the econometric analysis and the case studies.

ALTERNATIVE EXPLANATION 3: DOMESTIC INDICATORS

The organization and composition of domestic interest groups and the role of government–business relations can have an impact on policy adoption. The political system within each state (and sometimes a region) may either encourage or discourage the participation of interest groups. For example, the number of veto points in an economy could have an influence on the adoption of telecom regulatory reform, although the predicted direction is mixed. Countries could either reform less quickly because of a status quo bias enforced by domestic interest groups, or they could reform more quickly because of a need to signal a commitment to a competitive investment climate. It is difficult to test the effects of political leadership, government attitudes toward foreign direct investment, or cultural characteristics of the governance climate in the econometric analysis. These types of more embedded effects will become more apparent in the specific case analyses.

CONTROLS

Some of the hypotheses include country income and country size (population), which are known from diffusion literature to have an effect on the spread of policy reforms. Also, some international market measures include the degree of interconnectedness with the world economy, measured through the degree of international trade interdependence (the sum of exports and imports as a percentage of gross domestic product [GDP]) and the degree of capital market liberalization, using the International Monetary

Fund (IMF) Annual Report on Exchange Arrangements and Exchange Restrictions (AREAR) scale (explained in more detail in Chapter 3). These factors are included as general control factors for the force of international markets.

The rest of the book will help answer the question of why we have observed so much liberal telecom reform over so short a period of time by analyzing the timing of reform through an econometric analysis, in order to test the hypotheses specified by the theoretical framework. Next, to delve deeper into the actors and mechanisms behind this vast spread of liberal reform, we will analyze two case clusters of European countries. The case analysis follows a "most similar" research design stratified by income and country size, in order to hold constant some of the explanatory variables and reveal different policy and regulatory outcomes, especially in the area of privatization and the effectiveness of regulatory reform.

CHAPTER 3

When and How Do Countries Change the Rules?

Econometric Analysis of the Timing of Establishing Independent Regulators and Privatizing Telecom Firms

Some of the arguments about how globalization may have travelled around the world, and how global markets interact with government regulation in telecommunications, focus on sweeping global trends and specific country case studies. Further studies analyze the empirical effects of telecommunications liberalization in market infrastructure developments. Yet, what is missing is a way of structuring the analysis to ask, in a systematic way, how global markets, international institutions, and domestic politics may affect the timing of domestic institutional innovations. I argue that membership in international organizations is a critical factor in explaining domestic regulatory reform in telecommunications, in the context of globalization, Europeanization, and great technological change.

This chapter employs econometric analysis of 184 countries over the course of twenty-three years to analyze liberal trends in telecom reform, specifically when countries established a new, separate telecom regulator and when countries launched a first privatization effort.[1] By including many countries and a sustained time period in a systematic analysis, it is possible to move beyond the descriptions of the trends – namely, the 158 new regulators and 131 privatization efforts shown in Chapter 1 – and analyze whether it is possible to

[1] The overall project includes liberalization and re-regulation as part of telecom reform, but because of problems of cross-national data coverage in time-series format, they are not included in this chapter.

observe consistent patterns and variations while controlling for alternative explanations. With statistical analysis, it is possible to test the hypotheses outlined in Chapter 2 and also to account for the role of time, a key component of this research question.

Why did so many countries establish these regulators and privatize their telecom firms? The conventional wisdom emphasizes the role of international markets, big actors, domestic politics, and international policy diffusion. After discussing each of these factors, I will demonstrate that they fail to explain why and when countries enact these reforms. I then argue that the missing piece of the puzzle is the role of international organizations and how these organizations help states make their decisions to liberalize telecoms. I argue that international organizations are key actors and forums for the diffusion of the new telecom regulatory regime. International organizations help create and shape preferences for reform and also provide forums for expert discussions and the emergence of policy standards within the new regime for telecom regulation. Furthermore, I show why some international trading organizations (the World Trade Organization [WTO] and the Organization for Economic Cooperation and Development [OECD]) are more salient in the diffusion of telecom reforms than are others. This has not been shown in previous statistical analyses.

On the surface, it appears that liberal telecom reform is an excellent example for diffusion arguments, especially given both the S-shaped curve of policy reforms and the vast proliferation of reforms around the world. Several diffusion variables were created to measure the prior reforms in a country's peer group, and there was a strong bivariate association with diffusion variables and the timing of reform. Yet, when other theoretically important covariates were included, the diffusion effects disappeared and none emerged as statistically significant. This does not rule out a policy diffusion explanation, but it does suggest that it is necessary to create better measures to tap into this implicit underlying process.

This chapter has four parts. The first part presents a brief descriptive overview of some of these trends and variations, and a more detailed description of the specific variables to be measured. The second part presents the hypotheses derived from the theoretical framework in Chapter 2 and the specific statistical models to be used, both the Nelson-Aalen hazard model and the multivariate Weibull model. The third part presents the results and a brief discussion, and shows the variation between the process of establishing a separate regulator and privatization. The fourth part concludes with the main findings of the chapter and outlines steps for further analysis.

DEPENDENT VARIABLES

Two of the key dependent variables in telecom regulatory reform are the timing of establishing a separate regulatory authority for telecommunications and the timing of the first effort to privatize the dominant telecommunications incumbent. As shown in much greater detail in Chapter 1, these are two fundamental characteristics of market-oriented regulatory reform in telecommunications and reflect distinct patterns and variation within the overall trend toward global, market-oriented reform in telecommunications. Comparing and contrasting these two domestic policy innovations helps explain the extent to which policies diffuse around the world and indicates some of the limits of diffusion arguments. Both of these dependent variables entail substantial adjustments to the previous regime for regulating telecommunications.

DEPENDENT VARIABLE 1: SEPARATE REGULATORS

A separate regulator for telecoms entails first a separation of functions and powers between the government and the incumbent telecom operator. In many countries, the dominant telecommunications firm was owned, operated, and regulated by the government itself. The establishment of a separate regulatory office represents one of the first moves toward shifting government out of direct operation and management of the firm. This variable therefore measures whether or not a country has established a new regulator separate from the incumbent telecoms operator and the relevant government ministry (usually transport and communications). This indicator is drawn from the International

Telecommunications Union (ITU) regulatory survey and is based on whether the respondent indicated that the regulator is independent in terms of finance and authority. Although this measure is rough – it is based on the self-report of the regulatory authority – it still provides an indication of whether a country is enacting a reform of its regulatory institutions. Each country observation on the dependent variable is coded 0 for each year of the study until the year in which the separate regulator is established, in which case the country is coded 1 for that year.

DEPENDENT VARIABLE 2: FIRST PRIVATIZATION EFFORT

This variable measures whether or not a country has launched its first privatization effort of its state-owned telecom operator. This indicator is drawn from the ITU regulatory survey and is based on whether the respondent indicated that the government had privatized its incumbent. Each country observation is coded 0 for each year of the study until the year in which the government privatized the telecom incumbent, in which case the country is coded 1 for that year. Countries that enacted reform in a given year drop out of the set in the following year, creating a progressively smaller "risk set."

More than seventy countries introduced some degree of private sector participation in the predominantly state-owned incumbent telecom operators during the 1990s. By the end of 2001, 107 incumbents had at least partial private sector ownership, whereas eighty-three remained fully state-owned.

EXPLAINING THE TIMING OF TELECOM LIBERALIZATION

Building on the more extensive theoretical hypotheses expressed in Chapter 2, the specific hypotheses to be tested using this data are listed below.

- *Hypothesis 1: International organizations.* Countries that are members of international organizations will be more likely to adopt separate telecom regulators and may be more likely to launch privatization efforts through a mechanism that could be either competitive or emulative.

- *Hypothesis 2: International markets.* Countries are sensitive to changes in international prices for telephone calls, and thus changes in the international accounting rate will affect the timing of liberal telecom reform – increases in the accounting rate could lead to faster adoption of regulatory reform.
- *Hypothesis 3: Domestic politics.* Countries with more political constraints (veto points) may be more likely to enact market-oriented reform than those with fewer political constraints.
- *Hypothesis 4: Crisis and response.* Countries experiencing an economic crisis or financial difficulties are more likely to reform their telecom regulations. More specifically, countries with higher debt levels may be more likely to privatize in order to raise direct revenues. Also, countries with higher debt levels will be more likely to establish separate regulators in order to signal their commitment to the investment community that governments will not play an active role in managing the incumbent.
- *Hypothesis 5: Diffusion.* Countries will be more likely to enact market-oriented reform when other countries in key peer groups enact reform. Some key peer groups, based on other research mentioned in Chapter 2, include global numbers, regional peers, peers within income groups, neighbors, and peers within membership of particular international organizations.[2]

DATA MEASUREMENT

Data included in the analysis are presented in Appendix E. I use data from two primary sources to analyze both the timing of regulatory reform in telecommunications, as measured by establishing separate regulators for telecoms, and by launching a first effort to privatize the dominant telecom incumbent. First, the International Telecommunications Union (ITU) compiles telecommunications data for every country around the world. The

[2] A measure for trade-weighted peer groups, although desirable, is not currently available in country-year format.

ITU also conducts regulatory surveys every year, and, starting in 1999, the surveys list which countries have a separate regulatory authority and the year it was established, as well as a whether and when a country has privatized its incumbent telecom firm. I also include information on region, income, indebtedness, and foreign direct investment collected from the World Bank (WB) Development Indicators. For more specific telecom data, I utilized data published by the U.S. Federal Communications Commission (FCC) on international accounting rates and net settlements payments (FCC 2004). In addition, I utilize data from a number of different sources for international organizations (membership in the WTO, the OECD, and other regional trade agreements) and political variables, including regime type (Polity IV), political institutions (Beck et al. 2001), political constraints (Henisz 2000), and legal heritage (La Porta et al. 1997).

The dataset covers 184 countries, from 1970 to 2003, yielding a panel dataset with 6,324 observations. For this chapter, I focus primarily on this time period because it captures the dynamics of when most countries began to introduce competition into the market, as well as introduce other types of reform. Furthermore, not much was happening in 1975, and although there were some further institutional reforms after 2003 (see Appendix A and Appendix B), this period provides a good sample of the timing of reform. Appendix B provides a list of countries that established a separate regulator, privatized the incumbent, or both, including years for each event. I include summary statistics and descriptions of all variables in Appendix E. All independent variables are lagged one period to address concerns of possible endogeneity.

INTERNATIONAL AND DOMESTIC VARIABLES

International market factors are measured as a country's interconnectedness with the global economy through trade (a country's imports plus exports as a percentage of gross domestic product [GDP]) and capital openness (a country's ranking from 0–9 in terms of the openness of its capital account, based on International

Monetary Fund [IMF] Annual Report on Exchange Arrangements and Exchange Restrictions [AREAR] ratings).

International organizations are measured by membership in the General Agreement on Tariffs and Trade (GATT)-WTO and membership in the OECD in a given year. Although the European Union (EU) is modeled as an important factor in the overall project, in this global analysis, it is too collinear with the region "western Europe" to distinguish separate effects.

Sectoral performance is measured by the number of telephone mainlines per 1,000 people, and also by a telecom performance variable that is the ratio of the number of customers waiting for the installation of mainline telephones to the number of customers with phones, as suggested by other scholars (Henisz, Zelner, and Guillen 2005). A high value of the telecom performance variable indicates a clear performance shortfall and thus possible pressures for reform.

Interest group pressure is measured by two proxies, the percentage of the population living in urban areas and foreign direct investment (FDI) inflows as a percentage of gross domestic product (Li and Xu 2002). These are imperfect measures, but reflect the degree of urban consumers as demand for telecommunications services, as well as the extent to which a country depends on FDI inflows. Countries with a high percentage of urban consumers may be more likely to enact regulatory reform. The effect of FDI pressure is mixed, however. Countries with low levels of FDI may seek to attract more FDI, and thus reform to boost these levels. Alternatively, countries with high levels of FI may be less likely to change current status quo policies. Either way, the expectation is that an association will exist between FDI inflows and the timing of reform adoption.

To test the possibility of global policy diffusion, I created six diffusion variables that measure the global number of prior reforms (separate regulators or first privatization efforts), and number of prior reforms within regions, within income categories, within the WTO itself, and within the OECD. Each diffusion variable was created in the same way, and "region" is one example. First, I sorted the countries according to region-year and created a measure of the proportion of separate regulators (or first privatization efforts) within these region-years. I then subtracted the observation itself to obtain a score per country per year within this peer group. Each variable was lagged by one period, and the expectation is that countries will be affected by the decisions of other countries within the peer group (region) in the prior time period. The first measure is the "count," and I also created a separate measure for the proportion within the peer group that had innovated in the prior year. Diffusion hypotheses posit that the greater the number or proportion of separate regulators or privatization efforts in a prior year within a country's peer group, the higher the probability that a country will choose to enact a similar policy. The assumption behind these indicators is that policy-makers face uncertainty and bounded rationality, and thus they take into consideration the decisions of their peers when they search from a range of possible policy options.

CONTROLS

A set of control variables capture country-specific effects. The natural log of population and per capita GDP account together for a country's size and level of development. These controls are key indicators of a country's telecom market, and, as mentioned earlier, it is well-established that per capita income and a country's development of its telecom sector are highly correlated (Röller and Waverman 2001).

I included a set of regional dummy variables, using the WB classification of eight regions (East Asia-Pacific, Europe/Central Asia, Middle East/North Africa, South Asia, Western Europe, North America, Sub-Saharan Africa, and Latin America/Caribbean). My analysis controls for the effect of time by including dichotomous time variables for each year (Singer and Willett COMP: 1993). Since time-dependence is explicit, other time-varying explanatory variables (e.g., prior number of adoptions) are not contaminated by a larger variable of maturation effects. I also included dummy variables for four time periods, marking the substantive time periods of interest. These variables are wave1

(1934–1987), wave2 (1988–1992), wave3 (1993–1997), and wave4 (1998–2003).

To analyze the timing of the adoption of separate regulators for telecoms, I employ event history analysis, which is designed to study the patterns and causes of event occurrences (Allison 1984; Strang 1991; Yamaguchi 1991). Each country *X* is at risk of adopting reform in each time period *t*, until the time of adoption. The rate of transition from one state (the status quo) to another (policy adoption) is a function of covariates. The general form of a hazard models is

$$h(t) = \rho\lambda t^{\rho-1}, \quad \lambda = e^{Xjt\beta}$$

where h(t) is a hazard function for the policy reform to transition from nonadoption to adoption at time *t*, with observed covariate row vectors X_{jt} and parameters to be estimated ρ and β (Blossfeld and Rohwer 2002; Hosmer and Lemeshow 1999). A graphical depiction of the hazard estimate is depicted later, with the Nelson-Aalen estimate, as well as a description of the Weibull model chosen for the multivariate analysis.

The hazard function is defined as the probability of enacting regulatory reform (by creating a separate regulator or launching the first privatization effort), given that the country has not yet enacted such a regulatory reform. I estimated Weibull models, which state that the probability or "risk" of establishing a separate regulator for telecoms or privatizing the incumbent is a function of diffusion and international and domestic factors.[3] These models incorporate international market factors (trade and capital

[3] I also estimated a Cox model, which does not make as many assumptions about functional form as the Weibull. If the model is specified correctly in each case, the coefficients and the direction of the hazard should be similar in both models. The Cox regression is a semi-parametric method that can fit data without having to specify a functional form (e.g., a baseline or increasing hazard). The hazard is expressed in a ratio and the baseline drops out; the effects of the covariates are estimated relative to the characteristics of the time-varying risk set. The Cox model does, however, make a proportional hazard assumption, which assumes that all countries have a proportional hazard of establishing separate regulators. Results were consistent with the Weibull and thus are not reported.

openness, international accounting rates for telephone calls), and membership in international organizations (WTO, OECD), and domestic factors (debt service, political constraints, urban consumers, and telephone performance). I also tested a series of diffusion variables for country peer groups based on region, income group, and membership in international organizations.

Expectations

I argue that membership in international organizations, particularly liberal trading organizations, increases the probability that countries will liberalize their telecom sectors. Also, membership in liberal trading organizations can affect the speed and timing of reforms, as some reform more quickly than others.

Of the 183 countries under analysis, 129 countries established separate regulators and 102 countries launched first privatization efforts. The remaining countries are regarded as "censored" because we do not know when or whether they will establish separate regulators. Censoring can pose a problem in the analysis due to unobserved heterogeneity, in that those countries that were especially likely to establish separate regulators might reform early, which might bias the analysis (Box-Steffensmeier and Jones 2004).

Yet, we do know that the majority of countries liberalized their telecom sectors during the 1990s, and even more countries liberalized in the early 2000s, almost reaching a global saturation point. The starting date of 1975 was selected for the model since the first official telecom reform occurred in Chile in 1977, and the first wave of telecom reforms occurred in the United States, Britain, and Japan in 1984. By selecting a starting date for the hazard model earlier than these events, it is possible to capture some of the elements that may have led to these early reforms, as well as the bulk of later reforms occurring in the late 1990s.

Results are shown in the Appendix F. All results are measured in hazard ratios, and if the coefficient on the hazard ratio is greater than 1, it indicates an increasing hazard, meaning an increasing chance of establishing a separate regulator for telecommunications or launching a first privatization effort. If the coefficient is less than

1, it indicates a decreasing hazard, which means a decreasing risk of establishing a separate regulator for telecoms. Hazard ratios can be understood as the change in the odds of policy adoption associated with a one-unit change in the explanatory variable. Therefore, hazard ratios larger than 1 represent an increased probability of policy adoption; of 0–1 a decreased probability of policy adoption; and of 1, no effect. For reasons of space, I will explain the hazard ratios for only three of the variables in the results table, found in Appendix F, which explain the timing of the adoption of a separate regulator.

The variable OECD member has a hazard ratio of 1.83 in the separate regulator model, which means that *ceteris paribus*, a one-unit change in a country's adoption of a separate regulator increases the probability that a country will adopt a separate regulator. The hazard ratio for "trade" across most model specifications is about 1.0, which indicates that there is no relationship between a country's trade dependence and the timing of liberal reform. The hazard ratio for income per capita in the separate regulator model is 1.15, which indicates that the lower the income per capita, the higher the probability that a country will enact regulatory reform.

The first important result is that membership in international organizations emerges as significant in explaining the timing of reform for both establishing a separate regulator and for privatizing the incumbent, but the results vary across reform. Membership in the WTO increases a country's probability of adopting a separate regulator by a hazard ratio of 2.69. This makes sense substantively, in that having a telecom regulator separate from the incumbent was one of the general principles of the WTO Basic Agreement on Telecommunications, adopted in 1997, and most member countries established new agencies either before or after this deadline. Membership in the WTO also has a positive and statistically significant impact on the timing of privatizing the incumbent telecom operator, with a hazard ratio of 1.88, less than that of establishing a separate regulator. This result also makes sense substantively, in that private ownership of a telecom incumbent was not a requirement for the market access commitments of the WTO Basic

Agreement on Telecommunications or other documents relating to telecommunications, as was establishing a separate regulator.

Membership in the OECD does have a positive and statistically significant effect on both establishing a separate regulator and privatizing the state-owned incumbent, with hazard ratios of 1.83 and 1.90, respectively. This result is interesting, in that the OECD made best practice recommendations for the creation of separate regulators, but did not have a specific set of recommendations for privatization.

DISCUSSION

In sum, there are liberal trends across countries, especially in the establishment of separate regulatory agencies and privatizing state-owned telecoms companies. Overall, the most important variables to emerge from these models are membership in the GATT and the WTO and membership in the OECD. In the privatization model, a country's income and size are two important predictors, although membership in the OECD, as indicated by the large hazard ratio of 2.61, shows great significance in the timing of privatizing the incumbent.

A country's trade dependence, as measured by the sum of imports and exports as a percentage of GDP, shows a hazard ratio of 1 across all model specifications, with no statistical significance. These results indicate that trade dependence does not have an effect on the timing of regulatory reform in telecommunications. Substantively, it is not surprising that the direct link between trade dependence and timing of telecom regulatory reform is weak and tenuous, although we might expect there to be more of an influence, given not only the shift in telecoms as a tradable service but also a country's overall integration into the international economy. Still, it is possible that trade is not as important as we might think, at least in terms of the timing of regulatory reform.

A country's ranking of capital openness also hovers around 1, and is sometimes statistically significant in the models for establishing a separate regulator, which indicates that a country's capital openness has either no effect or a mildly positive effect on the timing of establishing a separate regulator. This makes sense substantively, in that we would expect that having an open capital account would also indicate a country's openness to portfolio investment in telecommunications or direct investment in telecommunications, both of which might be affected by the status of the capital account. Also, having an open capital account might indicate a government's overall willingness to open up the economy to investment and trade. The small hazard ratio and occasional statistical significance support this mild association between capital openness and timing of regulatory reform.

One signal to the broader investment community that a sizeable investment in telecommunications is not at risk of government expropriation of assets is to establish a separate regulator for telecommunications, thus indicating that the government no longer plays a direct role in the operations and regulation of the telecom incumbent. Another strategy for the government to attract FDI inflows is by launching a first privatization effort. Yet, although the signs of the hazard ratio are appropriately negative, the models do not yield statistically significant results, and thus we must continue to explore these hypotheses in other work.

The most important findings, however, are that country commitments to the WTO and OECD have a substantial influence on the timing of domestic institutional reform, particularly the establishment of a separate regulatory agency. I also posit that creating these institutions at the same time as joining the WTO (and, for some countries, the OECD) signaled a commitment to market liberalism and the overall consensus that competition and markets was both desirable and could bring great financial and investment gains. All countries, for example, had been members of the ITU, but the wave of reforms happened once the debate over telecommunications regulation was shifted over to the WTO, when telecoms and electronic communications became a tradeable service with investment potential. Clearly, the descriptive statistics show that it was necessary in the first wave and even the second wave of reforms that major international actors pushed the agenda of market-opening measures, namely the United States. Yet, it was also interesting when developing countries opted to sign the Basic

Agreement, as shown in Singh's terrific analysis of the WTO negotiations (Singh 2008).

CONCLUSION

The traditional stories of telecom regulatory reform are not satisfactory as they are not able to identify the specific causes, actors, or mechanisms behind this vast convergence in market reforms. Although conventional wisdom holds that international markets and domestic politics determine when a government chooses to liberalize its telephones, this study shows this conclusion to be incorrect. Instead, I show that international organization membership is the single most significant factor that varies across policy areas.

Having a telecom regulator separate from the incumbent is one of the requirements for signing the WTO Basic Agreement on Telecommunications, and we would expect countries to have a separate regulator. Yet, what the data do not show is why countries chose a particular form of separate regulatory agency, as this form is not stipulated as a requirement for the WTO commitment or for EU membership. Thus, it is necessary to move beyond the data and the traditional stories of telecom regulatory reform in order to identify the specific actors and mechanisms behind this vast convergence.

The diffusion approaches that are becoming more popular in the literature provide interesting insights, but their concepts and measures do not perform well in the econometric analysis for this study of telecom reforms. For example, identifying regional patterns of reform is helpful, but what characteristics of regions determine why some regions are more innovative and others are not? Furthermore, some of the broader notions of global policy diffusion, as currently constructed by the proportion of prior adoptions within a peer group identified by the analyst, are more suggestive than conclusive, especially without attention being paid to the overall specific motivations of policy-makers. Also, in this analysis, the more general measures of diffusion did not produce results that were as powerful as in other settings. This partly may be due to some conceptualization and measurement issues in the data. It could be that a diffusion approach is more of an empirical regularity in search of a theory. Yet, another alternative is that diffusion is more deeply embedded than depicted and measured in this work, as well as in other studies.

Theoretically, the combination of international, domestic, and diffusion factors in an analysis of policy innovation helps provide a more complete understanding of how the world works, and how to navigate the tenuous and increasingly blurred boundary between international and domestic politics.

In terms of policy implications, it has become clear that having a separate regulatory agency has become *de rigueur* for most countries around the world. Even some of the most heavily regulated and government-owned economies have started to spin off separate regulatory agencies. Also, although there appears to be an ideological consensus that having a regulator separate from the incumbent is necessary, and having a regulator separate from the ministry is desirable, it is not apparent why that must always be the case.

It appears that membership in international organizations, especially the WTO and the OECD, is pivotal in determining the timing of the new telecom regime, as opposed to most traditional arguments about global markets, domestic politics, and domestic economic factors. Why would this be the case? I argue that countries take part in international socialization through membership in these international organizations and others. The OECD in particular is important because of its peer-reviewed regulatory studies. The EU is another group that is important in determining the shape of the regulatory regime. Although it is difficult to show the European influence in the current statistical analysis, it is clear that European directives on the Information Society were important for countries in adopting new regulatory agencies for the information society and also for liberalizing their telecom regimes.

As developed in Chapter 2, one signal to the broader investment community that a sizeable investment in telecommunications is not at risk of government expropriation of assets is to establish a separate regulator for telecommunications, thus indicating that the government no longer plays a direct role in the operations and regulation of the telecom incumbent. Another strategy for the government to attract FDI inflows is by launching a first privatization effort. As discussed earlier, privatization of the telecommunications incumbent is one of the flagship privatizations for many governments around the world and could be a direct response to the low level of other FDI inflows. Yet, although the signs of the hazard ratio are appropriately negative, the models do not yield statistically significant results; thus, we must continue to explore these hypotheses in other chapters.

For example, an important event in the market for global telecommunications is that of the global downturn in telecom investment, which occurred when the bubble crashed around 2000. I included possible indicators for a global telecom market variable that would show this shock to the marketplace from speculative efforts in the auctions of spectrum and third-generation (3G) wireless technology in Europe and large bankruptcies in telecom firms such as Sprint/Global Crossing, all of which are beyond the scope of this chapter. I included a measure for total global revenue from telecommunications (equipment and services), as well as global number of mainlines, mobile phones, global telephone traffic, the number of internet users, etc. Yet, none of these variables yielded statistically significant results in any of the model specifications.[4]

The analysis also included a battery of other possible omitted variables that could influence the timing of regulatory reform, including the level of democracy (Polity IV), ideology of the political leadership (right party in power), and two other measures of debt (short-term debt and debt service as a percentage of exports). The inclusion of these other variables does not substantially alter the results, although they do reduce the number of observations in the sample size. Regional and year dummies

[4] Data are drawn from the ITU World Telecommunications Indicators 2002. Results available upon request.

were also tested, but did not emerge as significant. Results are available upon request.

As suggested by the OECD variable in both models, the OECD seems to have played an important role in the timing, substance, and direction of telecom regulatory reform in the case studies of Chapters 4 and 5, particularly through its peer review of telecom regulatory reform. Furthermore, although the OECD surveys and research reports on regulatory reform strongly recommend the establishment of separate regulatory agencies, this is not an official requirement for countries to follow.

Whereas Western Europe and the region of Central Europe revealed trends in reform, it was not possible to analyze how these reforms spread, at least in the context of the current models. In the case chapters, it is possible to analyze the role of specific European actors, institutions, and networks in the spread and variation of telecom reform, particularly in light of EU directives, accession, and networks of cooperation.

Strengths of Mixed-Method Research

One of the main strengths of employing econometric analysis in so many countries over time is the ability to draw conclusions about how membership in international organizations plays a much stronger role in the timing of domestic institutional innovations in these countries. It is possible to generalize over time and space, painting a broad-brush picture of how global trends unfold and how some traditional explanations for telecom reform do not compete with other, external factors (e.g., membership in key liberal international trading institutions).

What the analysis does not, however, reveal is the range of actors and mechanisms by which these processes unfold on a global, regional, or domestic level. Using these broad conclusions and suggestions, it is possible to dig deeper into more qualitative, historical, and institutional analysis to investigate how these processes play out – or not. The case chapters from Central and Northern Europe provide an excellent example of how and when membership in international institutions mattered in the adoption of domestic institutional innovation, and how it was more through networks of diffusion – information networks, harmonization networks, and networks of regulators themselves, and through mechanisms of emulation, mimesis, competition, and some forms of coercion in terms of membership access – that reforms were undertaken.

CHAPTER 4

Regulatory Reform in Central Europe

Freer Markets, European Rules

This chapter explores some of the key trends in liberal telecom reform highlighted in the quantitative analysis, and it analyzes some of the key actors and mechanisms behind the overall trend in liberal reform. In so doing, it obtains a better picture of how reforms travel around the world and of the key dynamics of these new markets and government actors in the realm of telecommunications.

Some of the main findings of this chapter are that policy-makers are influenced by the behavior of other countries and institutions through specific international organizations – the European Union (EU), the Organization for Economic Cooperation and Development (OECD) – direct bilateral ties with regulators in other countries, indirect examples of other country models, and ties with countries through large foreign direct investors. The four countries – the Czech Republic, Hungary, Poland, and Slovakia – are frequently compared and are often referred to as the "Visegrad 4," referring to the close cooperative efforts between the four countries since the early 1990s.

Interaction with international organizations and experts helped push these countries toward a common trend of market-oriented reform, but each country chose a specific national path toward establishing a separate regulator, harmonizing regulations with the *acquis*, and privatizing the main telecom operator, according to domestic political and economic institutions. Although there is a high degree of convergence in the forms of regulation, there is continued divergence in the implementation of telecom reforms.

After a brief contextual presentation of telecom market structures and shifts toward telecom liberalization in the Visegrad 4, this chapter is organized in four parts (1) explaining key similarities (diffusion through key international organizations, technological change, presence of foreign investors), (2) key differences in reform (preferences for foreign direct investment [FDI], no norm of privatization, main political considerations), and (3) country-specific stories of regulatory reform. The chapter concludes with a summary of the findings.

This chapter shows that pure technological pressures and a simple coercion model of accession to the EU are necessary but not sufficient in explaining the similarities of outcomes. This chapter also shows how political and economic configurations – namely, government preferences for FDI – affect decisions to privatize the state-owned incumbent.

The findings of this chapter complement some of the other literature of postcommunist political and economic reform, which studies the politics and economics of pension reform (Orenstein 2001), corporate governance (McDermott 2002), central bank independence and North Atlantic Treaty Organization (NATO) accession (Epstein 2008), central bank embeddedness in the Czech Republic and Hungary (Johnson 2006), mass privatization programs (Appel 2004), EU accession and administrative reforms (Grzymała-Busse 2002), and state-building (O'Dwyer 2006).

Some rationalist studies of postcommunist countries have shown that conditionality mechanisms based on material interests explain domestic political change, especially membership conditionality in joining international organizations, when domestic opposition to the policies is low (Kelley 2004; Schimmelfennig and Sedelmeier 2005; Vachudova 2005). Yet, other scholars have shown that conditionality imposed by international organizations has limited or no effects on domestic policies (Barnett and Finnemore 2004; Weyland 2006). Some argue that the mere geographical proximity of Central and Eastern Europe to the EU is a predictor of political and economic change, independent of causal influences flowing from the organization itself (Kopstein and Reilly 2000). In the context of minority traditions, Jacoby shows that international actors deploy material resources to domestic actors into order deploy an ideological agenda in a "coalition approach" (Jacoby 2008).

Some examples of the "varieties of capitalism" literature, as applied to postcommunist central Europe, argued that states pursued multiple paths of privatization and thus multiple types of capitalism (Stark and Bruszt 1998). Other analysts have argued the importance of domestic institutions, including constitutions. Frydman and Rapaczynski make an interest-based explanation, stating that political constraints on neoliberal privatization decision making stem from de facto control of enterprises by managers, workers, or state interests (Frydman and Rapaczynski 1994). In my research, I find that manager or worker control does not appear as a central explanation for the privatization of telecommunications firms. In the four countries in this study, I find more substantial evidence for state-led market-oriented reform in general, and varied degrees of privatization depending on political preferences.

SHIFTS TOWARD TELECOMMUNICATIONS LIBERALIZATION IN THE VISEGRAD 4

The Czech Republic, Hungary, Poland, and Slovakia are postsocialist middle-income countries that faced challenges of transition to a market economy and democracy; they are known as some of the more successful countries in Central and Eastern Europe in terms of economic and political reform. Neoliberal explanations of reform in all countries at the time of reform did not mention much about the role of the state, but rather stressed the importance of private property (Blanchard et al. 1991). As stated earlier in this book, the neoliberal story of shifting to a market economy was cast in the light of introducing private property rights to previously state-owned markets. If countries could get the property rights in the hands of private investors – domestic or international – then markets could bring prosperity and growth. In terms of overall economic reform, Poland pursued "shock therapy" (Sachs 1993), Hungary had a more gradual approach, and the Czechs were somewhere in between. Slovakia followed a path similar to that of the Czech Republic's but with key variations, particularly in the role of populist political leaders.

All four countries have enacted some degree of liberal regulatory reform in the telecommunications sector. The four main aspects of liberal regulatory reform in telecoms include liberalizing market segments (lifting restrictions to entry and lifting quotas on licenses), introducing private sector participation into the sector by selling shares of the incumbent to the public and/or a strategic investor, introducing new regulations for competition (re-regulation), and delegating authority to new regulatory authorities separate from the incumbent telecom operator and then later to regulators independent from both the incumbent operator and the ministry.

Although some analysts have provided descriptions of telecom development in the region as a whole, they have not provided a synthetic analysis of the countries in the region, particularly in the context of globalization and EU enlargement (Sallai, Schmideg, and Lajtha 1996; Stern 1994; Welfens 1995). Other analysts have focused on economic developments within the telecom sector through 1999 and during the period of the global telecom boom of the early 2000s (Bruce, Kessides, and Kneifel 1999), whereas others focused on economic development prior to 1995 (Heller 1994; Newbery 1991; Nulty 1994). Although these empirical studies are valuable, they do not synthesize some of the main political forces converging both from the outside as well as within the countries, which highlights the importance of international institutions and norms as well as domestic policy variations.

The Visegrad 4 countries are part of the larger trend of liberal reform in the telecommunications industry and, although domestic political and economic configurations certainly play a role in explaining how policies are enacted and the degree of reform effectiveness, this analysis focuses more on the possible external factors that influence liberal regulatory reform in telecommunications. By choosing these four similarly situated countries that seem particularly susceptible to external influences for regulatory reform, it will be possible to specify the paths through which globalization, EU accession and participation, and policy diffusion may travel. Also, although all countries enacted liberal reforms, they vary especially in the privatization plans of their telecom incumbents, and this provides insights into the limits of external and diffusion arguments.

TELECOMMUNICATIONS CIRCA 1989: ANTIQUATED INFRASTRUCTURE

Communist regimes were never known for promoting communications among people, and these regimes bequeathed inadequate telephone systems to their fledgling democratic successors. The sheer volume of calls from newly established businesses regularly overwhelmed the entire exchange. An OECD survey in 1993 showed that substandard telecommunications was Eastern Europe's most serious infrastructure obstacle to exports. In addition, the antiquated phone system deterred foreign investors in the early years of reforms. General Electric, for example, blamed part of its 1992 loss at its Tungsram lighting company to the cost of establishing microwave links to its plant in Nagykanizsa, in western Hungary (Denton 1993).

All countries faced extremely decrepit infrastructure in the basic backbone, the network, and the quality of lines, as well as reduced availability of phones and service. For example, in 1991, more than 60 percent of the telephone exchanges in Czechoslovakia dated from the 1950s. In Hungary, much of the equipment was installed by the Bell Telecom Company in the 1880s, and, in many rural areas, telephone service stopped entirely after 4:00 PM, when the operators of the manual switches went home Denton 1993). In all four countries, less than 15 per 100 people had access to a mainline phone in 1991, and wait lists for a phone often extended beyond ten years (International Telecommunications Union [ITU] 2010).

All four countries desperately needed a cash infusion to modernize their networks and bring the telecom infrastructure into the twentieth century (Madden and Savage 1998). One of the first overarching goals in all four countries was to expand, modernize, and digitize the network, and to boost telephone penetration levels to around 35 percent by the year 2000, still below the OECD average at that time (43.3 percent) (OECD 2011).

Each of the four countries had a dominant incumbent and fixed-line network. Also, each country faced competitive pressures in the fixed market from the mobile market, particularly after 1998, as new mobile companies competed with the sluggish incumbents on price, quality of service, and wait time. Some participants observed that "the only technical advantage which the Czech Republic has in telecommunications is that we have to rebuild the infrastructure almost from scratch" (Mihal Cupa, head of the strategy section of national operator Czech Telecom, in Denton 1993).

LIBERAL REFORM IN THE VISEGRAD 4

All four countries first spun off a separate regulatory office from the state-owned incumbent, thus fulfilling the first step toward creating a separate regulator. Most countries established these separate regulatory offices within a ministry, either the Ministry of Economy or the Ministry of Transport and Communications. All four countries, however, then took the next step of establishing a regulator independent of the dominant line ministry, and most established independent regulatory agencies around 2000.

All four countries had legally independent regulatory agencies by 2000, yet all share another similarity; namely, that formal independence did not necessarily mean actual independence from either the dominant incumbent or the government itself. For example, only the Hungarian Communications Authority was self-financing as of 2002, whereas the rest of the "independent agencies" were still financed out of the government budget, in addition to the collection of licensing fees. The four countries made further adjustments to their regulators, in line with the EU regulatory framework of 2002 and subsequent amendments of 2009.

Some liberal reform – the lifting of barriers to entry and to licensing in market segments – began in the early 1990s. Countries began to grant licenses to alternative operators as early as 1991, and, in the Czech Republic, for example, the number of fixed-line licenses for the national market jumped from 1 to 33 by 2001 (OECD 2001).

Yet, although granting licenses and opening some barriers to licensing is one form of liberalization, some of the more challenging aspects involve re-regulation, which raises questions about how to regulate operators with significant market power (SMP) and how to promote a more competitive market, as will be discussed later. Furthermore, some countries have taken more steps than others both in advancing the liberalization of the market and in re-regulation, as will be discussed later (Xavier 2000). For example, some analysts have described the 1990s in Poland as a "lost decade of liberalization" because regulations favored the incumbent operator (International Center for Economic Growth 2003).

In Eastern Europe, the debate about deregulation or re-regulation had a different meaning, as the entire economy of the region was controlled by the state, allowing no degree of competition. In addition, there was no experience with regulating any kind of competition, let alone regulating "for competition." None of the European investors had much experience with competition in utilities either, although arguably they had more than in Eastern Europe.

All four countries introduced legislation on telecommunications at several points during the past two decades of reform. All four introduced a Telecommunications Act between 1990 and 1992, and then again in 2000, 2002, and now 2009 (European Commission 2009). Some of these legislative changes included specific considerations for competition regulation, and, in the later iterations, included the creation of an independent regulator. The legislation was designed to open market segments to competition, create a regulatory agency that could design and enforce regulation, and introduce a new way of regulating the entire sector for telecommunications and then electronic communications. This process was challenging for all countries; for an excellent overview of how these changes are negotiated in developing countries, Wilson and Wong provide a terrific account of negotiating the internet in Africa (Wilson and Wong 2007).

Yet, some of the more challenging aspects of telecom sector re-regulation, especially the policies of interconnection agreements and universal service obligations, were postponed. These issues were part of the 2002 EU framework on electronic directives, as amended by the 2009 revised directives on better regulation and the consumer protection directive, as discussed later in this chapter.

All four countries faced a mandate to introduce regulations in terms of licensing, tariff rebalancing, interconnection, universal service obligations, and more. Also, all four experienced turf battles between their ministries of finance in terms of tariff rebalancing and spectrum management, and their ministries of transport and communications with nascent regulatory authorities.

Some observers have argued that "a failure to find the right balance between de-regulation and re-regulation contributed to creating conditions that culminated in the 1997 currency crisis (in the Czech Republic) and helps explain the country's slow growth since then" (OECD 2001).

In Central Europe, some of the main trends over the past ten years are the continued dominance of the incumbent in fixed telephony and broadband, and usually a major presence in the mobile communications market. Although mobile markets are mostly competitive, the major players have substantial international backing. For example, T-Mobile in the Czech Republic is owned by Deutsche Telekom, which also owns shares in Slovak Telecom in Slovakia (incumbent), Matav in Hungary (incumbent), and other operations throughout Europe. In terms of regulatory highlights, there are continued concerns on the part of the European Commission, among others, about the actual independence of the national regulatory agencies (NRAs), as well as about the resources and regulatory capacity of these regulators.

In many countries around the world, the type of convergence that has emerged in telecommunications is less concerned with markets appearing identical, and more with how large market players have started to provide multiple platforms of service, including wireless, wireline, and broadband.

On an European level, at the time of the first introduction of liberalization in 1998, and then in 2002, the activities of civil society were limited. Although there were provisions for universal access to basic voice telephony and discussions of access to the internet, there was very little included in the package about inclusion of civil society in the response to regulation, as well as in dispute settlement with the telecommunications regulators. This has changed after the 2009 updates to the framework for electronic communications regulation, as two of the major amendments to the European framework include what are known as the "better regulation" directives as well as the "consumer services" regulations.

I argue that this represents a learning process whereby institutions and political groups acknowledge the inherent need for better market regulation, as well as the difficulty of regulating markets for electronic communications, given the need for technical expertise of regulators and lawyers, and the preponderance of market resources held by large incumbents. For example, much of the regulatory staff from Slovakia was drawn from the former state Ministry of Transport and Communication and might be skilled technically in analogue technology, but from an older technology, nonmarket perspective. How could these regulators operate against a team of business advisors from Deutsche Telekom, who worked with the incumbent firm to negotiate issues of interconnection and who were experienced with a range of markets, technologies, legal strategies, and operations?

PRIVATIZATION

Although all four Visegrad 4 countries raised the issue of privatization and made plans for eventual privatization, only Hungary was quick to enact this program and completed the full privatization of its telecom incumbent as early as 1993 (Newbery 1991). The other three countries were slower: the Czech Republic launched its first privatization effort in 1995, bought back shares, and then privatized again ten years later, in 2005. Slovakia and Poland followed in 2000. All countries considered the options of introducing some kind of private sector participation into the dominant state-owned incumbent, as well as into the growing mobile industry.

Privatization was often hailed as the great solution to the transformation of former socialist economies, and countries across the region began selling off state assets. The theory was that by getting property rights in order, market participants would then have the incentive to be more competitive and efficient (Megginson and Netter 2001; Roland 2000; Vickers and Yarrow 1988). Yet, as the

OECD notes in the case of the Czech Republic, "The privatization program did not always produce the competitive and efficient firms that were expected, partly due to lack of proper regulatory and legal frameworks" (OECD 2001). Other scholars went further, denouncing the neoliberal ideology of privatization that became the "politics of greed," as privatization structured politics and institutions in Central Europe (Schwartz 2006).

A telecom incumbent's privatization is a signal of great importance to the domestic economy, where state-owned firms are usually the largest employers and prominent on the domestic stock market. As important, selling off strategic stakes in formerly state-owned monopolies to Western companies was seen across the region of postcommunist Eastern Europe as both a source of needed finance and the best way to gain access to new technology needed to upgrade domestic networks and integrate with the global economy. In addition, upgrading this technology was a key component for creating a competitive business environment. Telecommunications was seen as one of the key tools for bringing the formerly isolated, postcommunist countries into the global economy, and privatization of the telecom incumbent was often the flagship of a government's overall efforts to transform and modernize its economy. Some analysts felt that telecom privatization "should help encourage the whole privatization process and foreign capital inflows [to the region]" (Charles Frank, EBRD first vice-president, in Done 1998).

All four countries introduced some degree of private sector participation into the sector, and, although the plans and degree of effort varied (as we will see later in the chapter), all four countries emphasized privatization over competition in the early stages. For example, all four countries granted monopoly concession agreements to the dominant incumbents and as part of the overall privatization process.

In Hungary, as opposed to the Czech Republic and Slovakia, early democratic governments established a regulatory regimen to monitor privatization decisions, which prevented banks and enterprise managers from striking special deals or stripping assets from the state (Barnes 2003).

EXPLAINING KEY SIMILARITIES ACROSS VISEGRAD 4: INTERNATIONAL ORGANIZATIONS AND TECHNOLOGICAL CHANGE

Although all countries began programs of liberal telecom reform, they received many pressures and incentives from international organizations to lead the way toward this liberal market reform. Clell Harral, of the European Bank for Reconstruction and Development, said that "multinational institutions such as the OECD and the European Commission should step up their co-ordination of efforts to help former communist nations develop independent telecommunications regulators" (Marsh 1995).

Hanley also argued for the role of critical international agencies, especially the International Monetary Fund (IMF) and EU, in promoting private ownership in Hungary through FDI (Hanley, King, and János 2002).

Diffusion Through International Organizations and Networks

The main channels of diffusion for telecom regulatory reform in the Visegrad 4 countries were through information networks (especially the OECD, but with some through the European Bank of Reconstruction and Development [EBRD]), some harmonization networks (especially the EU, but with some through the World Trade Organization [WTO]), and regulatory networks (Independent Regulators Group [IRG], European Regulators Group [ERG], Body of European Regulators of Electronic Communications [BEREC], and networks of European regulatory authorities).

Diffusion Through Information Networks

In the case of the Visegrad 4 countries, channels of diffusion through information networks traveled particularly through the OECD and the EBRD, and less through the larger organizations of the International Telecommunications Union (ITU) and the

World Bank (WB). This is shown more clearly in the descriptions below.

European Bank for Reconstruction and Development

Telecom development in Central and Eastern Europe was seen as one of the keys to modernizing the economies of these formerly communist countries. The EBRD committed one-tenth of funds since its foundation to the telecom sector.

Organization for Economic Cooperation and Development

All Visegrad 4 countries joined the OECD. The Czech Republic became a full member of the OECD in 1995. Three of the four countries – the Czech Republic, Hungary, and Poland – were asked by the OECD to undergo a series of peer reviews of the state of regulatory reforms and governance, particularly in the telecommunications sector, after 1997. These reports were prepared by teams of researchers and government officials, and were peer reviewed by other OECD countries. These reports are now available on the OECD website, and they provide a descriptive analysis of the current state of the market, as well as prescriptive advice for future policy reform (OECD 2000b, 2001, 2002a).

Both the Czech and Polish sites express a conviction that joining the OECD was similar to joining other large international organizations, in that "by joining the OECD in 1996, Poland was seeking to better integrate itself into global policy making circles. It was also gaining access to a wealth of experience from the OECD Secretariat and policy makers in its member countries" (OECD 2002a). All four countries joined large international organizations, signed on to commitments to democracy and introducing market reforms, and signed on to the principles of free trade.

International Telecommunications Union

Although all countries participated in the ITU, as did most other countries in the world, it is not clear that ITU meetings and commitments were the driving force behind regulatory reform here. The resources provided by the ITU and the World Dialogue on Regulation can be valuable for policy-makers and regulators as reference points and as chances to interact with other experts in meetings. Yet, interviews in Central Europe in 2002–3 revealed that policy-makers and regulators were more focused on obligations to the EU and the WTO.[1]

Diffusion Through Harmonization Networks

The second subtype of diffusion through international organizations occurs through harmonization networks, in which more conditionality is placed upon entrance, as well as more obligations and commitments once a country becomes a member. The EU, WTO, and IMF are all intergovernmental organizations that involve a substantial degree of commitment in trade, finance, and other areas of harmonization.

International Monetary Fund

Many scholars have studied the (potential) coercive relationship of international agencies, especially the IMF, on domestic politics within transitional and developing countries, particularly through the mechanism of conditionality for membership or for provision of funding (Stone 2002).

World Trade Organization

All four countries joined the General Agreement on Tariffs and Trade (GATT) prior to 1994, and thus were able to be founding members of the WTO at the time of its inception in 1995. All four countries signed the Reference Paper on Telecommunications and agreed to liberalize their telecommunications markets. One of the conditions for the Reference Paper was the establishment of a regulatory authority separate from the operating agency of the telecommunications firm, and, eventually, all formed regulatory agencies separate from the operating function of the state-owned firm. This was not, however, a condition for acceding to the

[1] Interviews with policy-makers in the Czech Republic, Hungary, Slovakia 2002–3.

WTO. Further, there were no penalties launched against the countries for not having an independent regulatory authority for telecommunications, at least not through official WTO channels and its dispute settlement mechanism. Therefore, it seems highly unlikely that the conditionality and coercive effect of the WTO was directly responsible for the pattern of liberal reform over time in the four countries of postcommunist Europe.

Finally, the domestic political institutions responsible for forming some of these international commitments – namely, the ministries of foreign affairs – were not tied directly to the policy-making arms for telecommunications – namely, the ministries of transportation and communications. The link is tenuous at best that these particular ministries were communicating with each other about these issues. More likely is that the overall ideology of liberal reform, promulgated from the highest levels of government, contributed to the overall shape and contours of liberal reform. Yet, although this can explain some of the general nature of reform, political and strategic issues set the structure for other reforms (e.g., the kind of privatization processes, the kind of licensing auctions, and the specific strengths of the telecom regulator).

The European Union

In explaining policy choices and outcomes, many analyses argue that the EU played a critical role as an external force. The EU included overall conditions for the development of a market economy and liberal democracy as criteria for accession, and telecommunications was one of the chapters included in the progress toward becoming a member of the EU. All four countries started formal talks with the EU shortly after the great changes in 1989–90 and joined the EU in May 2004. The EU not only set conditions for membership, but its Commission enacted assistance programs for many aspects of accession and development in a complex array of policies and institutional remedies. Although some observers would expect a particular EU template of reforms, the institutional and policy outcomes vary widely (Grabbe 2006).

On European Union Accession

In 1993, the European Council adopted the Copenhagen Criteria, in which member countries needed to attain a democracy and the rule of law, a functioning market economy, and fulfillment of membership obligations. Most of the Visegrad 4 countries attained this, with only Slovakia failing in terms of democracy and minority rights until 2003.

Telecom reform cannot be simply contingent on EU conditionality, because we observe great variation across countries in terms of privatization of their telecom incumbent, development and structure of the independent regulatory agency, degree of independence, and structure of competition. Some scholars have shown that the EU provided limited oversight and resources for the adoption of the *acquis* and certain sectors, so, although formal laws and regulations may have fulfilled the general criteria for being a market economy, these laws and regulations did not actually become functional (Jacoby 2004).

All four countries in the study acceded to the EU in 2004. Yet, by 2004, these states had already started their own pattern of liberal reform in telecoms, among other sectors. Therefore, if it is not strict coercion and conditionality from outside, the driver for reform must come from something within.

One of the main pressures for reform coming from the EU is through the adoption and implementation of the EU directives in telecommunications, with their goal of forming a single market in electronic communications. All four countries sought accession to the EU and began negotiating association agreements in the early 1990s. By the time they joined the EU in May 2004, this meant a clear commitment to harmonize domestic legislation and regulations with the current *acquis*. In the regular reports on progress toward EU accession, began in 1998, the relevant chapters in the *acquis communautaire* for telecommunications are chapter 19 on Telecommunications and the Information Society, chapter 3 on Services, and chapter 6 on Competition Policy (Commission of the European Communities 2003a, 2003b, 2003c, 2003d).

The transposition of directives and regulations for an internal market posed challenges for all four countries, especially as, during the 1990s, the EU changed its own regulatory framework on telecommunications. The accession countries began to work with the principles outlined in the 1987 Green Paper on Telecommunications reform, which projected an eventual liberalization of the telecom market (all market segments) by 1998 in all member states. Also, the EU introduced seven new Directives on Electronic Communications in 2002, under which telecom reform are subsumed, including the strengthening of a national regulatory authority for telecoms within each member state. As shown in Chapter 2, the EU also introduced amended packages on electronic communications in 2009 as well.

In terms of the establishment of separate regulatory authorities, legislation from the EU required member states to separate regulatory responsibilities from operational functions as early as 1990 (Article 7 of the Commission Directive 90/388/EC published in OJ NoL192, July 24, 1990). Yet, this was only clarified in subsequent legislation, in 1997 (Article 5a paragraph 2 of Directive 90/387/EC as amended by Article 1 paragraph 6 of Directive 97/51/EC published in OJ NoL 2195/23, October 29, 1997).

Some of the countries in the study have made much greater progress than others in adopting the *acquis*. Hungary was one of the quickest in terms of implementing telecom regulatory reforms and introducing liberalization measures. Most of the countries experienced serious legislative difficulty at some point during the process, including the hurdles of transposing the seven new EU directives. This transposition also requires each country to enact not only the directives themselves, but secondary legislation related to the directives, including measures for state administration, competition authorities, and more. All countries face challenges in moving forward with this process, and this is not confined to the accession countries. The European Commission recently launched an inquiry against France and other major European member states for their failure to transpose the directives on electronic commerce for 2003 and also for 2009.

Some of the common problems include the lack of experience in writing and enforcing telecom regulation and legislations, as well as hurdles met when encountering the legislature. Some of these regulations have not been tested anywhere, and all four countries face challenges in how to regulate a dynamic sector while still providing service for the public interest.

The EU's PHARE program is one of its three preaccession instruments designed to assist applicant countries of Central Europe in their preparations for joining the EU. PHARE's pre-accession focus was put into place especially after 1997, in response to the Luxembourg Council's launching of the accession projects. One of the key programs included "twinning," in which sector members, particularly regulators, were paired with regulators in EU member states to draft programs of regulatory reform and policies.[2] These ranged from short-term expert (STE) visits to longer term secondment of experts to the regulatory agencies of the accession countries, with expenses paid through the PHARE twinning office.

Each of the four countries had a different "twinner" through the EU's PHARE program. The Czechs worked with Dutch (Onafhankelijke Post en Telecommunicatie Autoriteit [OPTA]) and Spanish "twinner" regulators, and the Hungarians worked with Finland's NRA (Viestintävirasto Kommunikationsverket [FICORA]) and Portugal's regulators. The Poles worked with Britain's Oftel and with the Swedish regulator, and the Slovaks worked with British experts, the Danish regulator, and the Netherlands (OPTA). These twinning programs provided much information about possible paths toward regulatory reform, although these were often paths not taken. For example, interviews with government representatives reveal that some of the recommendations were not followed because of lack of political will, as well as because of lack of human resources and capacity within the new regulatory agency.[3]

The EU issued a report through PHARE in 1997 to make financial aid conditional on the progress of reforms. One of the accession priorities for Poland, for example, included a demand

[2] http://europa.eu.int/comm/enlargement/pas/twinning/index.html

[3] Interviews in Slovakia and Czech Republic in May 2003.

for a start to be made on privatizing Telekomunikacja Polska, the main telecom operator, as cited in Bobinski (1998).

Diffusion Through Regulatory Networks

The third subtype of diffusion through international organizations occurs through regulatory networks. The twinning program through PHARE provided one example of diffusion through regulator networks by providing bilateral and direct links between countries and their regulatory agencies. By partnering with firms and agencies in other European economies, it became possible to share ideas and experience about how to regulate the dynamic and unfolding market for telecommunications.

Another example of harmonization through regulatory networks is through the European networks of telecommunications regulators. All EU countries, including the Visegrad 4, joined the ERG, the IRG, and, later, the BEREC, as shown in Chapter 2. These meetings provided opportunities for regulators to interact with each other in closed and open forums, and to discuss how to regulate issues of cross-border provision of services, roaming, termination rates for fixed and mobile telephony, spectrum assignment and frequency rights, and other difficult pricing issues. The BEREC meets regularly, as structured through the EU, and also hears opinions from other market participants, including incumbent operators and alternative providers.

Most countries looked to overall examples of telecom development in the world, neighbors, and other EU countries with small, fragmented markets. As shown in the specific country case sections, Hungary looked to Finland and Portugal, and the Czech Republic looked to the Netherlands for examples, as shown in the country studies.

Horizontal Networks of Firms and International Interest Groups

The activities of multinational telecommunications providers from within their home country market monopolies to other countries can be characterized as another type of horizontal diffusion network. For example, when Deutsche Telekom of Germany invested in Slovakia and Hungary, among other Eastern European countries, it implemented many of the same kinds of policies in the host countries as in its home country, Germany.

As shown in the presentation of the telecommunications market structure, international telecommunications firms have scrambled to join the race to enter the market in Central and Eastern Europe. The privatization and sell-off of state enterprises in Latin America was already well under way, and the global telecom market began to see the emergence of large strategic alliances in search of global market share. All of the Visegrad 4 countries were considered to be attractive prospects, and most of the world's major firms swarmed like sharks in a tank. Some of the major players in Eastern Europe include Deutsche Telekom, France Télécom, British Telecom, the Dutch operator (later known as KPN), Swisscom, AT&T, Verizon, SBC, TeleDanmark (Denmark), Telia (Sweden), Telenor (Norway), and Sonera (Finland). Other new actors also emerged, namely new business associations and some elements of civil society.

Regional patterns of investment have emerged as the dominant incumbents on the European continent (namely, Deutsche Telekom, France Télécom, and Spain's Telefonica) have invested heavily in Central Europe. The Scandinavian companies have entered some of the Central European countries, but have invested heavily in the Baltic countries as well. A joint venture between Sweden's Telia and Finland's Sonera held a 60 percent share in the Lithuanian telco, 40 percent of the Estonian telco, and 49 percent in the Latvian telco (in OECD 2011, Communications Outlook for 2009).

In terms of investing operators, the largest player is Deutsche Telekom for fixed-line expansion, with joint ventures in Hungary, Slovakia, and Croatia. This company is also primed for investment in the Czech Republic, with its belated full privatization attempt. Deutsche Telekom formed an alliance with Ameritech (which later pulled out) and started to implement a regionwide strategy. Other participants in fixed-line telephony, which has only begun to be competitive despite the liberalization of fixed-line licenses in 1998, include Scandinavian companies. The Scandinavian incumbents formed alliances and invested throughout the region under the name of Tele, a combination of TeleDanmark, Telenor (Norway), Sonera (Finland), and Telia (Sweden) (European Commission 2010b).

In terms of mobile communications, Deutsche Telekom is also active through its own mobile branch, T-Mobile, which provides services in Western and Eastern Europe under its own name. In the Czech Republic, for example, the second largest mobile provider is now known as T-Mobile, second only to the incumbent (Telefonica O2 CR, formerly Eurotel) and a third mobile operator, Vodafone (formerly Oscar). France Télécom is also one of the more active large telecom investors in the region, particularly through its mobile branch of Orange. Orange provides services in Slovakia. France Télécom is also involved in Poland and Hungary. Some of the other larger European telco providers were once involved in bidding on tenders for fixed licenses (Stet Italia, Telefonica), usually in alliance with other multinational firms (European Commission 2009).

KPN of the Netherlands used to be extremely active in the Eastern European markets, with a joint venture and minority ownership of Czech Telecom, as well as significant interests in the Hungarian telecom market. KPN encountered financial difficulties, partly due to overleveraging on third-generation (3G) licenses in western Europe, and it sold most of its shares in 2001 and 2002. After several years, Telefonica of Spain won the competitive bid for the reprivatized Czech Telecom, and this company is now known as Telefonica O2 CR. In Hungary, KPN retained a defining stake in Pantel Company, an alternative service provider, but subsequently left the market.

One interesting note is that many of the companies that were pushing for market opening measures in the Visegrad 4 countries in the early 1990s were those with comfortable monopolies in their home countries (e.g., Deutsche Telekom, France Télécom, KPN). Some observers at that time noted "Ironically, the prospect of further telecoms privatizations in Eastern Europe may put even more pressure on Western governments to speed up liberalization of their own markets" (Boland 1995, p. 24).

New Actors

In all four countries, new actors within the overall telecom landscape have emerged and have fundamentally changed the markets. The first actors include alternative operators for telecommunications. In the Visegrad 4, any kind of private business was new in the telecommunications field, and, over the past twenty years, private sector activity has flourished with the establishment of internet service providers, mobile telephony, and other businesses. Other new actors include business associations, which sometimes include the incumbent operator and sometimes are groupings of alternative providers. Although all four countries experienced the emergence of local business associations and some consumer advocacy groups, the degree and effectiveness of these varied considerably across countries.

EXPLAINING KEY DIFFERENCES IN LIBERAL TELECOM REFORM

This section shows the enduring patterns of national regulation, in the context of overall globalization and Europeanization.

Enduring National Patterns of Politics and Economics

Foreign Direct Investment Versus Portfolio Investment

In *foreign direct investment* (FDI), a company buys actual shares in another company. *Portfolio investment* occurs when shares are traded on the stock market and opened to institutional and individual investors. One key difference toward increasing private sector participation in the market as a whole emerged around the issue of courting FDI versus portfolio investment and transfer of shares to domestic investors. There's a sense of "selling the family jewels" to foreign direct investors, who are much more visible, as opposed to selling minority shares to portfolio investors. Some governments, particularly those of the Czech Republic and Poland, sought more portfolio investors and often had great resistance to selling state assets to foreigners.

Many analysts argue that this is in part because of the success of voucher privatization as a whole in both the Czech Republic and Poland, as well as persistent strands of nationalism (Orenstein 2001). Some analysts argued that broader political reasons affected the Czech government's decision to choose telecoms from two small European countries in preference to the French-, German-, and Italian-led consortia bidding for Czech Telecom. The Czech government at the time seemed sensitive to dependence on Germany, in that "a leading role for Deutsche Telekom would reinforce Germany's economic influence, already uncomfortably large, over a country it occupied in the second world war" (Denton 1994). In addition, the government was wary of further involvement with France after a failed deal with Air France, and skeptical of Stet, the Italian telecom company (Robinson 1995).

Even in Hungary, arguably one of the most advanced economies and welcoming of FDI, the process of privatization and FDI was not without problems. Nationalism and the identities of the foreign investors proved to be important not only in choosing the key strategic investors for the telecom company, but also for other smaller firms. This was the case with Hungaraton and the sale of a Hungarian musical archive to Polygram, the world's largest music group, based in the Netherlands. Tamas Suchman, the privatization minister, claimed that the Polygram bid had been disqualified on technical grounds, but also expressed his pleasure that Hungaraton's archive "should not be transferred to foreigners" (Denton 1993).

The choice of favoring portfolio investment, however, had a cost, as became apparent when portfolio investors began a stampede to exit the markets of emerging economies after the Asian and Russian financial crises in 1997. Cash-strapped governments had often counted on privatization proceeds to cover budget deficits and government debt, in addition to helping with the challenges of infrastructure investment. Some of the skepticism can be found in a report from Nomura, a Japanese investment bank, which stated that "even with the prospect of EU membership down the line, some will not have the resilience to last the course. Investors should ask themselves whether certain institutions can survive long enough to enter 'German heaven'" (Done 1998, p. 3).

Foreign debt did not appear to be a general predictor of liberal regulatory reform in the Visegrad 4. Hungary and Poland started out with high levels of foreign debt, yet followed radically different paths to liberal reform. Hungary liberalized, privatized, and re-regulated the economy and telecommunications with more speed, comprehensiveness, and vigor, whereas the Poles focused on other economic issues and telecommunications stagnated. The Czech Republic and Slovakia had low levels of foreign debt, which may have partly explained why it took so long to privatize and introduce foreign investment, but it certainly does not explain all of it.

The domestic interest groups that often play a role in other countries in promoting or opposing liberalization, privatization, and competition in telecommunications were often absent in the countries of Central Europe. Labor unions were important in Poland during the process of telecom reform and privatization of the economy, but were not as important in the other three countries. In Hungary, for example, "all the big trade unions are either uninterested in privatization or they support them as part of necessary reforms. Hostility to privatization is basically absent because it is still an abstraction for most workers" (Mihaly Csako, sociologist and trade union activist, as cited in Denton 1993). Consumer associations began to develop, but the most important players seemed to be the dominant incumbent operators, alternative operators, and their international partners.

New Ministries for Czechs and Hungarians

The Czech Republic and Hungary established new ministries to enact the policy-making functions for telecommunications and electronic commerce. In the Czech Republic, the Ministry of Informatics was established in 2003, and in Hungary the Ministry of Informatics and Communications was established also in 2003. The Czechs consulted with the Hungarians in setting up their ministry.[4] Poland and Slovakia continue to enact policies from

[4] "The Czech Ministry of Informatics will be set up taking the Hungarian example into account on 1 January 2003" (press release, Hungarian Ministry of Informatics and Communications, Budapest, October 18, 2002).

within the Ministry of Infrastructure and the Ministry of Transport and Communications, respectively.

COUNTRY-SPECIFIC LIBERAL TELECOM REFORM

Czech Republic

The Czech Republic: The Globalized Good Soldier Schweik

One of the typically Czech characters from literature is the Good Soldier Schweik (Hašek 1930). Schweik is an affable fellow who happily cooperates with all of the foreign influences and powers, Austrian or German, and, although he agrees to follow orders, he always finds his own way of doing things. The Czech Republic, in the process of introducing liberal telecommunications reforms, follows this example by enacting all of the reforms as prescribed by international organizations, especially the EU and the WTO, but implementing them in a Czech style. For example, the privatization of Czech Telecom has undergone multiple phases with several different groups of foreign investors, and was privatized again in 2005 to Telefonica of Spain. The Czech Republic joined the EU in 2004, yet did not choose to join the Eurozone and retains an air of "Euro-skepticism," particularly in the person of reelected President Vaclav Klaus.

Main Market Developments

The Czech Republic has a population of 10.5 million people, a gross domestic product (GDP) of US$190.2 billion, and GDP per capita of US$18,200 as of 2009 (Central Intelligence Agency [CIA] 2005–2011, World Factbook for 2010). The major telecom operators provide bundled services and converged fixed-mobile offers. The incumbent, Telefonica O2 CR, has been established as a converged fixed and mobile operator since 2007. The biggest mobile operator by number of subscribers, T-Mobile, made acquisitions in the fixed residential market and can now provide nationwide coverage.

As of 2011, there are four telecommunications providers in the Czech Republic. These firms are T-Mobile Czech Republic,

Telefonica O2 CR, Vodafone Czech Republic, and Mobilkom (U: fon). All of these firms have sought licenses for third generation/fourth-generation (3G/4G) technology and invested heavily in network buildout in Prague and in the rest of the country. Of these firms, all have significant foreign investment and ownership. Key investors come from Germany (Deutsche Telekom), Spain (Telefonica), and England (Vodafone).

Telefonica O2 CR is the fixed and mobile company owned by Telefonica of Spain, when it acquired the former monopoly operator, Czech Telecom in 2005 for 82.6 billion CZK. Telefonica bought a 51.4 percent share from the Czech government, then launched a buyout offer that increased its stake to 69.41 percent. The remaining shares are in float. One interesting point of history is the troubled past of telecom privatization, the role of the Dutch telecom SPT, and the renationalization of the firm.

Other actors include broadband providers UPC Ceska Republika (cable company), GTS Czech and Dial Telecom (including Volny), and a host of other cable providers (37 percent). Digital subscriber line (DSL) technology is one of the more popular options, although there is a competitive market for cable television and communications, as reported by the two cable television associations (Association of Czech Cable and Telecommunications Operators [APKT] and the Czech Association of Competitive Communications [CACC]).

The Czech Republic started liberalizing the economy in the early 1990s, as part of the overall program of liberal reforms. The Czechs created a separate telecommunications regulator rather early on, by establishing an office in the Ministry of Economy in 1993. This office was sent to the Ministry of Transport and Communications in 1996, and, in 2000, the Czech Parliament enacted the Telecommunications Act, which created the Czech Telecommunications Office (CTU) as an independent entity. Its main task is to "accomplish and maintain a competitive environment for the telecommunications market and to provide for the protection of the telecommunications market, including the protection of telecommunications service users" (CTO 2003).

Regulatory Environment: Main Regulatory Developments

The Czech regulator, the Czech Telecommunications Office (Český Telekomunikační Uřad, CTU), was officially given a new mandate in 2005. The CTU has acted in the market by issuing licenses, carrying out market reviews and investigations, and resolving some disputes in relation to implementation of remedies. Some of the key developments of 2010 included an assessment of number portability and interconnection with the incumbent provider, Telefonica O2 CR.

The Czech telecom market is governed by Act No. 127/2005 on Electronic Communications and on Amendment to Certain Related Acts (Electronic Communications Act) passed in May 2005. These laws seek to simplify the market entry process for new market players by introducing general authorization and cancelling licenses. The acts promote universal service, lower prices for interconnection and for consumers, and increased competition. The legislation aimed to bring the domestic Czech market more in line with the European regulatory framework for the Electronic Communications sector, as outlined earlier. Other important legislation includes Decree No. 430/2005, which provides criteria for assessing SMP in relevant electronic communications markets and the Measure of General Nature No. OOP/1/07.2005.[5]

Yet, the effectiveness of the regulator is in question. A representative from the Czech Association of Business Providers mentioned that the CTU is weak, which hurts the overall competitive climate for telecoms. For example, GTS Czech and Contactel had interconnection problems with Czech Telecom, and they asked the CTU for assistance. But, under the 2000 law, the CTU could only assist after a violation has been demonstrated, so there was no resolution. After sixty days, CTU decided nothing, so Czech Telecom took the case to the courts, where it was buried. Just being involved in a court case has precedence over a CTU decision, and

[5] For more recent updates to electronic communications legislation and regulations in the Czech Republic, please consult http://www.ctu.eu/main.php?pageid=178 (accessed September 12, 2012).

thus the case was quashed. Several outstanding cases have been waiting for over a year, and, due to claims that the dispute settlement hearings include proprietary information, the hearings are closed to the public.[6] Both business associations expressed concerns about the strength of the regulator, particularly in terms of combating the dominant powers of Czech Telecom. Members from Czech Telecom also expressed concerns about the weakness of the regulator, claiming that alternative operators were not obligated to fulfill universal service obligations or network buildout requirements, and thus were not sharing the burden of providing public service.

The Czech Republic's commitment to the WTO in 1997 first included a guarantee of market access and national treatment for domestic and international data, telex, telegraph, fax, leased circuits, closed user groups, domestic mobile services, and video and audio transport services. The Czech Republic phased in market access and national treatment for domestic and international voice services in 2001, and adopted the Reference Paper.

Interviews conducted in the Czech Republic in 2003 revealed that an office in the Ministry of Interior was tasked with constructing and enacting regulatory reform across a wide range of sectors. After the OECD asked the Czech Republic to commit to a peer review of the state of regulatory reform, the government agreed. After the first report and round of questions, a separate office in the Government Office was created specifically for regulatory reform. This office is preparing a law on procedures for separate regulators across a wide range of sectors, and works closely with experts within the OECD, both researchers and other country members. This peer-reviewed process of information exchange greatly contributed to substantial changes in how regulations are constructed in the Czech Republic.[7] This could be seen as an example of policy learning.

[6] Interview with member of the Association of Czech Telecom Operators (AVPTS), March 2003.

[7] Interviews with Czech government representatives, May 2003.

In the Czech Republic, during the first phase of reform, policymakers considered the examples of prior regulatory reforms in the United States and the United Kingdom, market leaders in deregulation and privatization. Other models included Mexico and Argentina, as examples of privatization programs of the incumbent that brought in large amounts of revenue to line government coffers (Hrubý 1997).

Yet, interviews reveal that the Czechs considered themselves as "European" and wanted to look to examples closer to home.[8] In later phases, particularly when creating a new regulatory framework after 2000, Czechs looked to the examples of Denmark, Finland, and the Netherlands as models of "regulation light," as opposed to the more heavy-handed regulatory style of France and Germany, as this lighter style of regulatory intervention was seen to be more effective.[9] In addition, these were small peripheral European countries with dynamic telecom sectors, which the Czechs wished to emulate.

The Czech Republic, for example, has several new business associations, many of which prepare documents on the best practices used in other parts of the world to implement liberal reform. Two business associations include the Asociace provozovatelů telekomunikačních sítí (AVPTS, Association of Czech Telecommunications Operators)[10] and the Czech Competitive Association of Cable Operators (CCAC).[11] The CCAC sought a "light" regulatory environment under the new directives, more like Denmark and less like France and Germany. This means that licensing is only necessary in cases of scarce resources (e.g., spectrum) and not in basic provision of services.

The Czechs launched a broad scheme of small-scale privatization, as well as an ambitious voucher privatization program for large-scale enterprises. The transfer to private ownership was substantial, yet the Czech government tended to favor domestic

[8] Interviews with member of Czech Ministry of Informatics, May 2003.
[9] Interviews with members of regulatory task force in Czech Government Office, May 2003.
[10] http://www.avpts.cz
[11] http://www.cacc.cz

rather than foreign investors. In addition, the Czech government retained some strategic industries, including telecoms, as strategic assets. Telefonica of Spain purchased shares in 2005 and rebranded the company Telefonica O2 CR.

In the Czech Republic, the closed stance toward foreign investors was promulgated by the Rightist party of Klaus from 1992 to 1998. The initial Klaus government (1992–8) proclaimed the glory of the free market and the principles of Hayek and Milton Friedman, yet continued to allow cross-ownership of banks, industry, and government; allowed nonperforming loans of state-owned enterprises to continue on the books; and completely failed to enact transparent reforms in government. In this, the party is similar to other right-wing parties that preach a message of limited government, while increasing government spending. It is a message of "do as we say, not as we do." The Klaus government fell during the extensive banking crises and scandals of 1997, economic downturn, and rampant corruption and "tunneling" led by prominent party officials (Schwartz 2006).

When subsequent social democratic governments came into power in the late 1990s, they pushed through much more comprehensive regulatory reform and privatizations. The Social Democrats under Miloš Zeman and Vladimir Spidla introduced a series of economic policy reforms to redress the shortcomings of the Klaus regime and to boost the Czech economy. They enacted a radical shift to encourage foreign investment, transparency, sound banking, and a stable monetary policy. Although the first Klaus government did pursue the privatization of Czech Telecom, this privatization was incomplete, and, after several failed attempts, the government had to renew its efforts to sell off shares in the incumbent. The Social Democrats were in charge as the Czech Republic began to undertake more serious, far-reaching regulatory reform in telecommunications, including the 2000 Telecommunications Act, the formation of the Ministry of Informatics, and efforts to transpose the European directives on electronic communications, in preparation for accession in May 2004. The Czech Republic was able to complete much of this work, but harmonization is a moving target, as the EU also amended its directives on electronic communications in

2009, thus creating more work for the Czech Parliament and the regulators.

The politics surrounding the reprivatization of Czech Telecom played a strong role in how events unfolded. The privatization occurred amidst a collapse of the minority government and a Parliamentary vote of no-confidence in 1995. The Czech cabinet had to choose the winner of the privatization tender during a time when its hold on power was tenuous. The opposition Civic Democrats had opposed the use of a tender and preferred to sell through the stock market. Yet, the privatization process was indeed completed, bringing an infusion of investment money into state coffers (Anderson 2005).

There was considerable political discussion around the reprivatization of Czech Telecom, including within the government itself. Prime Minister Stanislav Gross, finance Minister Bohuslav Sobotka, and Martin Jahn initially preferred to privatize via the stock market, whereas the information technology minister Vladimir Mlynar called for a tender (Anderson 2004). Ultimately, the government chose to privatize via tender, which was won by Telefonica of Spain.

In conclusion, liberal reform in the Czech Republic included relationships with foreign advisors and international organizations, yet was driven by domestic politics and Czech-style institutions. The more important underlying ideology was the introduction of market liberalism and competition, spread through commitments to the OECD, EU, and other international organizations. The ideals of regulating for competition spread through membership in the regulatory networks, from the IRG and ERG to the BEREC. Yet, there continues to be room for domestic political variation in the substance and style of regulatory reform, particularly in terms of priorities of the state.

Hungary: The Csárdás Dance of Liberalization

As in other sectors of the economy, policy-makers in Hungary introduced liberalization of the telecommunications sector soon after the initial set of "dual transitions" to democracy and market economy (Bartlett 1997). The pattern and pace of liberal reform with foreign investment followed a rhythm similar to the famous Hungarian folkdance, the *csárdás*, which starts out a bit slow and then builds to a fast, rapid tempo.

Main Market Developments

Hungary's population is about the same as the Czech Republic, at 10 million, and with a GDP in 2009 of US$129.3 billion, representing US$12,900 GDP per capita (CIA 2005–2011, in World Factbook 2010). Hungary joined the European Union in 2004, and continues to use the Hungarian forint as its currency unit. It is not in the Eurozone, unlike Slovakia.

As of 2011, Hungary's total number of wireless subscribers eclipsed the numbers of broadband and fixed line subscribers. Wireless subscribers totaled 11.89 million, with a market penetration of 118 percent, as compared with 1.96 million (50 percent) for broadband and 2.278 million (58.4 percent) for fixed lines. Fixed-line telephony continued to see drops in growth and revenue, as consumers switched services to mobile telephony and other alternatives (European Commission 2009, Hungary).

Main Regulatory Developments

The National Communications Authority (Nemzetí Hírközlési Hatóság, NHH) is the national regulatory office of Hungary, along with the prime minister's office. This national regulatory authority (NRA) has seen significant layoffs; organizational turnover of staff, board members, and the president of the agency; and a significant shift of responsibility to the prime minister's office between 2008 and 2010, and then to the newly formed Ministry of National Development in 2010. By June 2010, the government submitted a legislative package that merged the NHH with the National Radio and Television Commission, and restructured the agency.

In November 2003, an Electronic Communications Act (Eht) was passed, replacing Act XL of 2001 on Communications. The new law was structured to reduce the power of the dominant fixed-line incumbent, Magyar Telecom (Matav, now known as Mtel).

The legislation was supported by executive decrees on references offers, interconnection, number portability, and frequency allocation, and was based on the EU's regulatory framework of 2002. Most of these provisions were in place before Hungary acceded to the EU in May 2004 (European Commission 2009, Hungary).

Between 2005 and 2010, there were a few infringement proceedings of the European Commission against Hungary in the electronic communications market, particularly in matters of the state's golden share in Mtel, universal service elements, and several others, but none resulted in any fines (European Commission 2010b, Hungary).

The legal and regulatory underpinnings changed significantly in 2010, with the new Fidesz government. Act C of 2003 on Electronic Communications was amended on August 11 by Act LXXXII of 2010, and further amended by Act CIII of 2010 on the amendment of Acts concerning media and communication, and again amended in December by CLVII of 2010, enhancing the protection of public registries belonging to public digital assets (European Commission 2010a). Hungary also enacted a new Media Act (Act CLXXXV of December 2010) on media services and mass media, and subsequently merged the NHH with media regulation. As of 2011, the body became known as the National Media and Infocommunications Authority (Nemzetí Média és Hírközlési Hatóság, NMHH). The president of this body is elected for nine years, with strong safeguards against dismissal. As of December 2010, an amendment to the Constitution gave the new NRA the right to issue secondary legislation (decrees) (Act CXIII of 2010, amending Act XX of 1949 on the Constitution of the Republic of Hungary).[12]

This reconfiguration of regulatory institutions also followed a more general administrative restructuring in Hungary as a result of elections. By April 2010, the FIDESZ-KNP coalition won 263 out of 386 seats in Parliament, receiving the two-thirds majority to amend

[12] For more recent developments in the communications market and regulations in Hungary, please consult http://english.nmhh.hu/ (accessed September 12, 2012).

major legislative acts. One of the larger regulatory challenges for the NMHH is developing a strategy for next-generation networks (NGN), broadband, and the regulatory treatment of cable.

Hungary stepped out of line with its EU obligations and partners when, in 2010, it introduced a "crisis tax" on three major sectors of the Hungarian economy – retail commerce, telecommunications services, and energy distribution. Although grounded in Hungarian law (the Act on Electronic Communications), competing operators and the EU launched inquiries into this practice in 2010–11 (European Commission 2010b).

In Hungary, the communications authority was first established as a state office in 1989, with the separation of the operator and the ministry. The state office was divided into two institutions – one for telecom and post, and the other for frequency management. These two institutions were joined in 1992, and in 1993 became the Hungarian Communications Authority (Hírközlési Felügyelet, Hif). The Hungarian Communications Authority became legally independent in 2001, after the passage of the Telecommunications Act of 2001, and it finances itself through licenses and fees.

In Hungary, interviews reveal that in the first stage of regulatory reform, policy-makers sought to combine Anglo-Saxon models with more continental models of corporate governance in telecommunications, which was reflected in the choice of the Deutsche Telekom and Ameritech joint venture for the strategic sale of the Hungarian telecommunications incumbent, Matáv. Other studies of regulatory reform included the United States and Canada, as well as the newer models of New Zealand and Australia, but the Hungarians considered themselves "closer to Europe."[13]

In terms of more specific telecom regulations, interviews in Hungary reveal that policy-makers sought to combine the examples of Finland and Portugal as a possible model for the Hungarian communications authority.[14] Portugal is a large country, a late-joiner of the EU, with low income and high investment needs. Finland had a local multiplayer market that covered small

[13] Interviews with Hungarian policy-makers, May 2003.
[14] Interviews with Hungarian policy-makers in Budapest, May 2003.

territories and needed regulation to cover local markets, which Hungary faced with its concession plan involving multiplayer local markets across the country.

The Hungarian initial commitment to the WTO included market access and national treatment for data, telex/telegraph, fax, leased circuits, and satellite services (other than public voice). Hungary phased-in market access and national treatment for international and long-distance public voice as of 2003 and local public voice as of 2004, both ahead of the other members of the Visegrad 4. Public land mobile service was initially limited to one operator for NMT 450 MHz and two operators for global system for mobile communications (GSM) until 2003. In other services, paging was limited to one analog operator and two for pan-European service until 2003. Hungary has no foreign ownership restrictions except a 75 percent limit for Matav and Antenna Hungaria Rt. Hungary adopted the WTO Reference Paper on Telecommunications. Like the Czechs, Hungary actively sought OECD membership, and entered the program for the review of regulatory reform, including telecommunications, in the late 1990s (OECD 2000b).

The Hungarians were much quicker to privatize the telecom incumbent and showed much more openness to foreign direct investment in general than did any of the other four countries in the region. The Hungarians at first only sought limited, strategic foreign investment, but when the costs of network buildout and infrastructure modernization became unwieldy, they reversed position; Hungary ended by selling most of its large state-owned assets to foreign firms (including the telecom incumbent, Matav), and subsequently was able to modernize its networks and provide even better service than other countries in the region.

The Jozef Antall government announced in January 1990 that 85 percent of privatization revenues would be channeled toward the repayment of state debt (MTI-Econews 1990), and it stated a goal to sell 25 to 30 percent of state-owned enterprises to foreign parties within five years (MTI-Econews 1991). In Hungary, the austerity program was led by the (formerly communist) Socialist and Liberal coalition parties, which embarked upon a reform program in 1995 through 1998, after their election in 1994.

This program included cutting state spending and the privatization of telecommunications, as well as the rest of Hungarian industry. This reform program was wildly unpopular. Whereas the center-right party of Fidesz Hungarian Civic Party stopped privatization and renationalized some industry during its regime in 1998–2002, the Socialists gained a reputation for sound, free-market-oriented policies (in *Financial Times* December 4, 2002, p. 2). The general election of April 2002 was bitter and divisive as the ex-communist Socialist party and the liberal Alliance of Free Democrats (SzDSz), led by Peter Medgyessy, regained power after the defeat of the center-right Fidesz party of Viktor Orban (EIU, Economist Intelligence Unit 1999–2010, see 2008, Hungary).

Poland: Big Bang, but Slow Privatization

Poland followed a general path toward liberal reform that was similar to that of other central European countries, yet different in that Poland pursued a "big bang" approach (Sachs 1993) to macroeconomic reform, yet a slower, much more gradual approach toward privatization, especially of the telecommunications firm Telekomunikacja Polska (ATPSA) or Polish Telecom.[15]

Main Market Developments

Poland's market size is much larger than its neighbors, with its population of 38 million. Poland's GDP in 2009 was US$430.6 billion, with a GDP per capita of US$11,300 (CIA 2005–2011, World Factbook 2010, for Poland). Poland is a member of the EU, but the currency is the Polish Zloty (the PLN).

Strong competition continued in the mobile market, including a fourth entrant, although the incumbent Polish Telecom/Orange retained dominant market share in fixed telephony. Fixed broadband penetration was 16.02 percent in January 2011, below the EU average of 26.56 percent. Mobile penetration was 110 percent

[15] For more recent information on the main incumbent firm, Polish Telecom "Orange," please consult http://www.orange-ir.pl/ (accessed September 12, 2012).

in October 2010, which is high but still below the EU average of 124.2 percent. Fixed lines and traffic volume have declined over the past years, as have revenues (European Commission 2009, Poland).

Poland had a total of 47.3 million wireless subscribers in 2011, representing 124 percent of market penetration. As with the other European countries, this number eclipsed that of broadband (5.3 million at 38.2 percent penetration) and landlines (9.5 million, 67.6 percent penetration) (European Commission, 2010b, Poland).

In 1990, the Communications Act transformed the Polish Post, Telegram, and Telephone company into two entities, Telekomunikacja Polska (TP) and Poczta Polska (the Post). The state monopoly on local telecommunications was abolished in 1992, and private local telecommunications operators were licensed to offer services on a regional franchise basis. The State Treasury took control of TP in 1997, and, by 2001, the Telecommunications Law of 2000 came into force. The following year, the Ministry of Post and Telecommunications (MPT) was dissolved and replaced by the Office for Telecommunications Regulation, and again by the Office for Telecommunications and Post Regulation (URTiP) in 2002. The legislature and ministry drafted the new law for electronic communications in July 2004, and the Office of Electronic Communications (Urząd Komunikacji Elektronicznej, UKE) replaced the URTiP in 2006.[16]

Local telephony was liberalized in 1992, whereas domestic long-distance telephony was liberalized in January 2002, and international telephony was liberalized in January 2003. Major players in the Polish market in 2011 include Orange Poland (partially owned by France Télécom, Polkomtel, Polska Telefonia Cyfrowa [T-Mobile Poland], P4 [Play], Centernet, and other players) (European Commission 2010a).

Orange Poland was formerly known as Polska Telefonia Komorkowa Centertel (PTK, Centertel), until September 2005.

[16] For most recent regulatory developments at the Polish NRA, please consult http://www.en.uke.gov.pl/ukeen/index.jsp?place=Menu07&news_cat_id=79&layout=0 (accessed September 12, 2012).

France Télécom sold its 34 percent stake in Orange Poland to TP in 2005, which made Orange Poland a wholly owned subsidiary of TP. France Télécom owns a bit less than 50 percent of TP. The TP Group provides bundled service in Poland, including fixed-line telephony, leased lines, radio, television, data, and internet. TP's wireless subsidiary, Orange Poland, has also moved into the fixed broadband arena.

Main Regulatory Developments

The EU digital scorecard indicates that there was more cooperation between the incumbent and the NRA – the Prezes Urzędu Komunikacji Elektronicznej (UKE) – after they signed an agreement in 2009 to guarantee nondiscriminatory treatment of alternative operators in providing wholesale access to services. In 2009, a large review of the Telecommunications Act of 2004 was published, which aimed to bring the Act within the regulatory framework on electronic communications in the EU. The European Commission thereby closed three infringement proceedings concerning the independence of the NRA, consumer contracts, and interconnection. The broadband law, outlined later, aimed to ensure access to electronic communications services in order to combat digital exclusion (European Commission 2010b, Poland).

In 2010, the Act on the Development of Telecommunications Networks and Services (broadband law) entered into force and provided principles for local authorities to undertake telecommunications activity, as well as general approaches for streamlining investment. The European Court of Justice had ruled in case C-522/08 that, although the national rules establishing a general ban on bundled services were not precluded by the regulatory framework, this was not allowed under Directive 2005/29/EC on unfair business-to-consumer practices, and thus the new Act takes these issues into account European Commission 2010b, Poland, p. 6).

The president of UKE sought to increase service availability and stimulate investments in infrastructure, and, according to the EU digital scorecard, the "NRA continued to be active and innovative in the approach to regulations. Operators welcomed the shift in UKE's regulatory focus and noted more openness toward their point of view" (European Commission 2010b, Poland p. 2).

Poland has experienced some difficulties in enforcing some of the EU's harmonized regulations. In 2010, the European Commission opened an infringement proceeding, as the Polish NRA (UKE) seemed to have the power to set rates using methodologies other than the cost-orientation remedies laid out in the European framework (European Commission 2010a).

There are two main actors in regulating the Polish market for electronic communications – the UKE and the Ministry of Infrastructure, which is responsible for legal acts and ordinances. A Minister of Telecommunications operates within the larger ministry, which has nineteen other ministries within it. The NRA is fully state funded and continues to experience difficulties in attracting suitably qualified staff because of limited resources (European Commission 2009, Poland, p. 310).

The Telecommunications Act, which entered into force in 2010, grants the responsibility for market definition to the president of the UKE, which gives this NRA (and not the ministry) full control over market analysis. The amendment introduced a fixed five-year term for the president and outlined conditions for his or her dismissal. The European Commission had opened an infringement proceeding against Poland because, prior to this amendment, the president of the Council of Ministers had unlimited power to dismiss the head of the IRA without having to provide reasons (European Commission 2009, p. 310). In general, Poland's telecom policy follows the regulatory patterns of the EU directives and the WTO for increased market liberalization.

In Poland, the Office of National Telecommunications and Postal Inspection was created in the Ministry of Posts and Telecommunications (now Ministry of Infrastructure) according to the Telecommunications Law of 1990. The Office of Telecommunications and Post Regulation (URTiP), was first established as an independent entity in January 2001, according to the Telecommunications Law of 2000.[17]

[17] The website of the Polish regulator is http://www.urtip.gov.pl

Poland's initial commitment to the WTO Basic Agreement on Telecommunications Services included market access and national treatment for local public voice (wireline), domestic and international data, international fax, cellular, pan-European paging systems, and international private leased circuits. Poland phased-in market access and national treatment for telex and telegraph as of January 1, 2000, and market access and national treatment for all other services as of January 1, 2003. Unlike other members of the Visegrad 4, Poland does have foreign ownership restrictions, which limit foreign ownership to 49 percent for international and domestic long-distance services, including cellular. Also, Poland issued conditions that public digital cellular had to be provided through the incumbent TPSA's international network until January 1, 2003. Poland adopted the Reference Paper on general principles of liberal market access.

The Poles pursued an overall "big bang" approach to privatization, as part of an overall economic reform package in the early 1990s (Murrell 1993). Poland had an extensive privatization program, yet saved many of its largest, most strategic investments for last. Poland continued to attempt to privatize TPSA, but seems to have missed out on the big race for strategic telecom investors. In 1998, the Polish government debated privatization strategies for TPSA, and weighed the options of issuing a public offer of shares versus courting a strategic investor. The Minister of the Treasury in 1998, Emil Wasacz, said that the proceeds from privatization would be used to finance Poland's pension reform and repay outstanding government debts to public employees and retirees (Bobinski 1999). Interestingly, there was not much mention made about how the TPSA planned to raise money for the vast infrastructure investment needed for network buildout. At that time, TPSA planned to spend US$4.5 billion to extend and modernize its network through 2000, and intended to raise over US$800 million through a foreign bond issue. Some analysts have argued that the Polish telecom market as of 2001 was characterized by precompetitive market maneuvering on the part of international and domestic capital in preparation for the privatization of Polish Telecom and eventual accession to the EU (Dornisch

2001). The Poles retained key assets – key "jewels" – including the telecommunications operator and other large utilities. The government was concerned that full liberalization of all telecom services might affect the share price of the incumbent, TPSA, at the time of the initial stock offering. Poland did not launch the privatization of the incumbent, TPSA, until 2000, and even then the government retained 35 percent of the shares, followed by France Télécom.

Political Infighting About Privatization

"Privatization first, then liberalization," according to Andrzej Zielinski, Telecommunications Minister of Poland (Bobinski 1996). Poland's decision about the privatization (or not) of its main telecom firm was highly politicized. The first stage of privatization was an initial public offering through the Warsaw Stock Exchange. The goal at the time was to stave off trade union and nationalist opposition to the privatization by providing individual Polish citizens and institutions the opportunity to buy most of the 15 percent of government shares on offer (Robinson 1995). The second phase involved seeking a strategic investor for the next portion of shares.

The Ministry of Communications, led by Tomasz Szyszko of the ruling Christian National Alliance, was known to support widespread liberalization, whereas the Treasury Ministry, led by Emil Wasacz and the rival Freedom Union, preferred to create favorable conditions for strategic investors (Reed 2000).

Slovakia

Slovakia pursued its own path to liberal reform and was one of the later reformers within the Visegrad 4. Although some of this variation can be explained by relationships with international organizations, most of it rests in the domestic polity of Slovakia. Slovakia is smaller than the other countries of the Visegrad 4 and had more challenges in its political leadership after the breakup of Czechoslovakia in 1993, particularly with the populist leader Vladimir Mečiar. Subsequent administrations have pursued more market-oriented reforms in general (Bútorová and Bútora 1995; Goldman 1998). Slovakia has retained its own small-country policies of regulation and has shown less innovation in terms of policies than Hungary and the Czech Republic, except in the critical adoption of the Euro as part of its membership in the Eurozone. Yet, Slovakia had an advantage in some ways, in that it was able to observe some of the mistakes made by the Czech Republic in terms of the delayed privatization of Czech Telecom, and the Slovaks were able to partner with Deutsche Telekom when Slovak Telecom was privatized.

Main Market Developments

The major liberalization of the wireline sector took place in 2003, as local telephony, domestic long-distance telephony, and international telephony were liberalized. Legislation introduced competition, but the first interconnection agreement was signed only later in the year. New entrants represented by the Association of Telecoms Operators (ATO) claimed that Slovak Telecom's interconnection charges included an unreasonable profit squeeze, in addition to other contested issues (fixed and mobile termination rates, number portability, etc.) (European Commission 2009, Slovakia).

Slovakia has undergone many changes in the past two decades since its independence from the Czechoslovak Federal Republic. The population is 5.4 million as of 2009, with a GDP of US$87.8 billion and a GDP per capita of US$16,000 (CIA 2005–2011, in World Factbook 2010, Slovakia). Slovakia is a full member of the EU since 2004 and has adopted the Euro as its currency since 2009, unlike its neighbors the Czech Republic, Hungary, and Poland.

In Slovakia, despite the economic downturn from the global financial crisis of 2008, the electronic communications sector performed relatively well in 2008–9. The major players in the market have shown their intentions to bundle a range of services, including fixed, mobile, broadband, and cable television. Mobile data traffic continues to rise, and the fixed voice market is still dominated by the incumbent, Slovak Telecom (European Commission 2009, Slovakia).

Two major market players (the largest mobile operator and the fixed incumbent via its mobile subsidiary) offer converged fixed and mobile services for broadband, voice, and television. Cable operators try to offer more bundles and fiber to the home. The revenue of the electronic communications sector for 2009 was 2.1 billion Euros, of which 1.4 billion was from the mobile sector and 458 million from the fixed sectors. Lower revenues were particularly noticeable in the fixed market (European Commission 2010b, Slovakia).

The total number of wireless subscribers in 2001 was 6.17 million, with a penetration of 113.8 percent. Broadband subscribers were 897,000, with a market penetration of 40.8 percent, and total fixed lines numbered 1.06 million, representing a 48.4 percent household penetration (European Commission 2009, Slovakia).

The main wireless provider is T-Mobile Slovensko (formerly Eurotel Bratislava and a unit of the incumbent Slovak Telecom), which had a monopoly in the sector from 1991 to 1997. The second major player is Orange Slovensko (partly owned by France Télécom), which entered the market in 1997. In a decision surrounded by controversy among bidders, Telefonica O2 Slovakia entered the market in 2006 and won a twenty-year license in several frequencies (EIU 1999–2010, for 2009, Slovakia).

Deutsche Telekom acquired a 51 percent share in Slovak Telecom in July 2000 for US$950 million. In 2006, Slovak Telecom adopted Deutsche Telekom's T-com brand in the fixed-line market and changed its name from Telecom to Telekom (the name Slovak Telecom will be used throughout this book). Slovak Telecom is 51 percent owned by Deutsche Telekom, with the remainder held by the Slovak government through the Ministry of Economy (34 percent) and the National Property Fund of the Slovak Republic (15 percent). In 2004, Slovak Telecom paid U.S. firms Verizon and AT&T Wireless for the 49 percent stake in T-Mobile Slovensko, and the merger was completed in 2010 (European Commission 2010b, Slovakia).

Main Regulatory Developments

The legislative framework for the Slovak telecom sector is governed by the Electronic Communications Law (Act. No. 610/2003), which entered into force in January 2004. This updated the Telecommunications Law of July 2000, which had created two institutions for the state administration of telecommunications – the Ministry of Posts and Telecommunications (MTPT) and the Slovak Telecommunications Office (STO), also known as the Telekomunikačný úrad Slovenskej republiky (TUSR). The Electronic Communications Law introduced several major changes to Slovak legislation to bring it into compliance with the European framework on electronic communications, including the mechanism for attributing SMP in various market segments.

The European Commission had determined a conflict of interest in Slovakia, because the ministry that financed the operations of the telecommunications regulator also owned shares in the incumbent telecom provider, Slovak Telecom. The government then transferred its ownership shares in Slovak Telecom to the Ministry of Economy, creating more distance between the regulatory and management functions of the telecom operator. In January 2008, the European Commission closed the case against Slovakia (European Commission 2010b, Slovakia).

The policy-maker for electronic communications in the Slovak Republic is the Ministry of Transport, Construction, and Regional Development, and it works to transpose EU directives into Slovak law. The Ministry meets with the NRA and industry in drafting the new laws.

Historical View

In Slovakia, the Slovak Telecommunications Office (STO) was established within the Ministry of Transport and Communications in 1993. In 2000, the Slovak Parliament enacted the Telecommunications Act, which established the STO as a legally independent entity. For Slovakia, policy-makers looked to the examples of Finland and Portugal because they are small countries in both the EU and in the North Atlantic Treaty Organization

(NATO).[18] Other country examples include Denmark, the Netherlands, France, and the United Kingdom, as well as other small European countries.

The government of Vladimir Mečiar favored domestic entrepreneurs in privatization deals (sometimes known as his "friends and family plan" of privatization), and failed to follow through on a decision, made in 1996, to begin the privatization of Slovak Telecom. Slovak Telecom was transformed into a joint stock company in 1999, and then prepared for privatization.

During the course of privatization of Slovak Telecom in 2000, the telecom minister, Gabriel Palacka, was forced to resign under allegations of cronyism arising from the granting of GSM mobile licenses and the selection of international investment banks to advise in the privatization of Slovak Telecom. The prime minister at the time, Mikulaš Džurinda, said that the problems were exaggerated and were not a product of corruption but of inexperience at staging, and that they had invited the organization Transparency International to monitor Slovak's privatizations (Anderson 1999).

In 1996, NM Rothschild, the U.K. investment bank, was selected to advise the Slovak government on the first phase of the privatization of Slovak Telecom, its flagship privatization. Rothschild was chosen from a short list of four banks and given the task of preparing options for privatization and regulatory and price changes. The first phase of the project was funded by the World Bank (Boland 1995). This project stagnated until 1999, after the Mečiar government left power. Vladimir Mečiar refused to be rushed into the privatization of Slovak Telecom, stating that "we must improve either economy or financial standing and then the price we could get for their privatization would be higher" (Done 1997).

Slovakia faced many challenges throughout the 1990s in its quest for economic and political transformation. In the arena of telecom reform, the country stagnated under the extended rule of former prime minister, Vladimir Mečiar. As of 1997, Slovakia

[18] Interviews with Slovak policy-makers, May 2003.

was considered the "black hole" on the map of Europe; it was not invited to join the EU or NATO, and it was generally lambasted for authoritarian policies and its treatment of minorities, especially the Hungarian minority and the Roma (Kelley 2004). The Social Democrats were elected in 1998, and, under the leadership of the coalition and Džurinda, Slovakia began a rapid program of liberal reform, including outreach to international organizations. Leaders began a program of more concerted effort to join the EU (Schimmelfennig, Engert, and Knobel 2003). The Slovak government was involved in the first stage of small-scale privatization while still part of the Czechoslovak Federation, and the Slovak government continued with voucher privatization in the first and second waves of reform after the split of the country. Yet, the process was rife with corruption, particularly under the leadership of former prime minister Mečiar and his crony capitalism. Mečiar had very little interest in privatizing Slovak Telecom before boosting its possible sales price; he stated that, "We must improve their [Slovak Telecom's] economy and financial standing and then the price we could get for the privatization will be higher" (Done 1997, p. 2).

The second largest group is Orange, in the mobile sector. The ownership structure has a majority ownership of Orange (64 percent), which is a consortium led by France Télécom. Other owners include AIG New Europe Fund and the EBRD. Orange received its first license in 1997 for a GSM 900 band, and later received a license for GSM 1800 in 1999. Orange began marketing under the current brand name in June 2002.

Eurotel gained its first mobile license in Czechoslovakia as early as 1991. Eurotel Slovakia has over 1 million subscribers; it is owned by Slovak Telecom (51 percent) and Atlantic West (49 percent), which is a joint venture of Verizon and AT&T.

In 2002, Slovak Telecom wanted to launch asymmetric DSL (ADSL) service. The alternative operators pressured the antimonopoly office to stop the pilot plan for ADSL. The antimonopoly office delayed, made no decision, and prolonged the process. One year later, they decided that Slovak Telecom could launch DSL – but the delay ended up hurting consumers and wasting a lot of time and money in legal fees, as well as opportunity costs for potential profits.

Orange and Eurotel have not brought many cases before the ITU, perhaps because they already have significant market power and they have more to lose. Alternative operators, however, have very little to lose, and they quite regularly challenge interconnection and other rulings, and try to get decisions decided in court.

International Organizations and the Diffusion of Networks and Norms

Slovakia joined the OECD relatively late, in 2000, compared with the other members of the Visegrad 4. Slovakia is a member of the WTO and made a commitment to adopt the Reference Paper of the Basic Agreement on Telecommunications Services. According to the WTO Agreement, the Slovak Republic has committed to open market access and national treatment for data, telex/telegraph fax, private leased circuits, paging, trunked radio, domestic mobile and PCS (excluding analog cellular voice), and closed user groups (not connected to the public service networks). Slovakia committed to market access and national treatment for all other services, especially local, long-distance, and international telephony, as of January 2, 2003.[19]

The Slovak Republic also applied to accede to the EU, and joined with the other Visegrad 4 countries in 2004. Slovakia switched from being a Euro-skeptic under the Mečiar regime to a much more pro-European stance, and voters agreed to join the Eurozone and adopt the Euro as their common currency. This represented an even deeper commitment to economic integration than in some other European countries, including neighboring Czech Republic, Hungary, and Poland, as well as in other countries in this study – Denmark, Sweden, and Finland. Only Slovakia and the Netherlands are part of the Eurozone, even though all other countries peg their currencies to the Euro.

Slovakia participated in a series of activities with the EU as a part of the accession process, including the PHARE program.

[19] http://www.wto.org/english/tratop_e/serv_e/telecom_e/telecom_e.htm

Telecommunications was not seen as a barrier to accession, as was the country's policies toward nationalities, particularly the Roma and ethnic Hungarians (Kelley 2004). Yet, telecommunications was and continues to be part of the overall *acquis*; and Slovakia joined the BEREC.

Under the EU's PHARE program, the Slovak Republic participated in a twinning program with the Netherlands. Slovakia is also a member of the European Conference of Postal and Telecommunications Administrations (CEPT) and the ITU. The policy-maker for telecommunications is the Ministry of Transport, Posts, and Telecommunications. Slovakia also has a growing number of business and consumer associations, including the Association of Telecommunication Operators (ATO), which was founded July 20, 2001, in Bratislava.

In 2009, the EU opened an infringement proceeding against Slovakia for its lack of regulatory independence, particularly the dismissal of the chair of the STO by the Parliament in 2008. These proceedings were closed in June 2010, after Parliament enacted amendments to national regulation about the rules for dismissing the chair and the vice-chair (European Commission 2010b, Slovakia).

CONCLUSION

This analysis of telecom regulatory reform in four Central and Eastern European countries over the past decade has shown that it is necessary to consider specific factors from the global and domestic levels of analysis, as well as the paths for the diffusion of policy innovation. The structure of the international telecommunications environment influenced not only the spread of international strategic alliances and investments in the countries of Eastern Europe during the boom years, but also presented key vulnerabilities during the years of market collapse, both through the direct effects on overleveraged investors (KPN in the Czech Republic and Hungary) and through the behavior of portfolio investors in publicly traded companies.

The EU figures prominently as a source of pressure for regulatory reform for those countries that seek accession, although it also presents a moving target and a test of each government's capacity for administration, legislation, and regulation. Although the WTO Basic Agreement on Telecommunications presented a challenge for countries to open their markets, most had already begun to establish separate regulators, and most retained monopoly concession rights at least through 2003. Thus, countries were not as affected by the actual agreement as might be expected on first glance. The EBRD played a large role in restructuring the sector through its direct investments, and the OECD played the role of more of a facilitator of ideas through its peer-reviewed reports on regulatory reform within the countries.

The countries of Central and Eastern Europe, upon entering the EU, have shifted toward a harmonization of directives with the rest of the EU, yet they maintain distinctive, national patterns of regulation and market performance. Furthermore, the regulators in these countries have the opportunity to share some of their experiences with other regulators in the Western European sector, which could have an effect on other markets in Europe. Rather than passively receiving wisdom from abroad, decision-makers within the countries of Eastern Europe continue to devise regulations and policies suited to their own markets, and will maintain these country-level distinctions.

Although these external constraints can help explain the general direction and extent of reform, it is necessary to examine more closely the political and economic configurations within countries to understand some of the key variations in regulatory reform. For example, governments varied across countries and over time in terms of attitudes toward foreign investment, ranging from more open (Hungary throughout the time period) to more closed (Poland and Slovakia). This played a role in structuring the environment for telecommunications investors, who often sought ownership of the flagship enterprise as a means of greater income and profits.

Whereas interest group arguments figure prominently in the literature on regulatory reform in developed countries, particularly in the United States and Western Europe, the concept needs to be adjusted for the countries of Eastern Europe during this period. The overall inexperience with a market economy and a nascent civil society did not provide the same context for interest groups or a groundswell "from below" in terms of regulatory reform. Instead, global strategic alliances joined forces with either incumbents or competitors and reenacted many of the same debates that take place elsewhere in the world (e.g., the prices for interconnecting networks, the responsibility for providing funding for universal service, etc.). In this way, global actors become domestic interest groups, but following regional strategies of lobbying and negotiation. This presents even more challenges for the new regulatory agencies. These agencies are widely known to struggle with independence and effectiveness, as incumbents regularly take them to court to challenge regulatory decisions.

During the early years of reform, many analysts stressed the importance of privatization in general and of telecoms in particular as being key to prosperity, economic growth, and the achievement of social goals of universal access to a telephone and the internet. In more recent years, the emphasis has shifted to one of competition, market access, and the need for market re-regulation. Over time, regulatory reform in all four Visegrad 4 countries began to reflect general patterns in regulatory reform rather than country-specific or postcommunistic ones. Some of these persisting, yet global, problems include how to regulate interconnection prices between operators with SMP and alternative operators, and how to provide universal service obligations in that guarantee access to telecommunications services to as many consumers as possible.

CHAPTER 5

Northern European Regulatory Reform

Liberal Reform Northern Style, "Regulation Lite"

The chapter lays out how policy-makers are influenced by the behavior of other countries and institutions through specific international organizations – the European Union (EU), the Organization for Economic Cooperation and Development (OECD), direct bilateral ties with regulators in other countries, indirect examples of other country models, and ties with countries through large foreign direct investors. Thus, although there is a high degree of convergence in the direction of liberal reform, there is continued divergence in the implementation of telecom reforms, and there is great variation in the actual extent of privatization of the main telecom firms and in the degree of competition among firms. Globalization and Europeanization does not equal homogenization. The key cases in this chapter are Denmark and Netherlands, two of the founding members of the EU, as well as Finland and Sweden, who joined the EU in a later wave of reform, yet prior to the Visegrad 4 countries discussed in Chapter 4.

After a brief contextual presentation of telecom market structure and shifts toward telecom liberalization in the northern European countries, this chapter is divided into four sections: the first explains key similarities (diffusion through key international organizations, technological change, presence of foreign investors); the second explains key differences in reform (preferences for foreign direct investment [FDI], no norm of privatization, main political considerations); and the third details country-specific stories of regulatory reform. The findings are summarized in a conclusion.

This chapter analyzes four small, high-income countries in Northern Europe. Although case selection proceeded according to income groups and country size, in order to provide a controlled comparison with the other countries of Eastern Europe, all four countries are known to be innovators and leaders in telecom liberalization, although in different ways. The chapter outlines some key trends in liberal reforms, especially the interaction of market and international institutions, and then shows how specific interaction with international organizations often helps explain the persistent variation across countries.

Next, the chapter provides a comparison of the four country case examples – the Netherlands, Denmark, Sweden, and Finland. Even in highly competitive markets, considerable leeway exists for countries to enact their own, distinctive policy choices. For example, there is great variation across these countries in their choice of separate regulatory agency – for example, three countries have separate offices within the telecom ministry, which is not a pattern generally recommended by liberal theory and other proponents of regulatory reform.[1]

Furthermore, although telecom firms are highly competitive, considerable variation exists in state ownership. Although Denmark fully privatized TeleDanmark and the Netherlands partially privatized KPN, the Swedes and the Finns retain considerable state ownership in their joint incumbent telecom operator, Telia-Sonera. Finally, the Scandinavian countries in particular stress the importance of social responsibility and consensus building, factors that are written into the mission statements of each of the separate regulatory offices, suggesting what some argue is a "Nordic model of governance" (OECD 2003). In another study, Campbell and Pedersen show how Denmark continues to maintain international competitiveness with high taxes, a large welfare state, and economic regulation (Campbell and Pedersen 2007).

After a brief contextual presentation of telecom market structure and shifts toward telecom liberalization in these four small

[1] Japan does not have an independent regulator, despite competition in the market. I thank an anonymous reviewer for providing this example.

northern European markets, I discuss how global pressures through international organizations and international markets help explain similarities in telecom reform by providing an orienting framework toward liberal reform and the establishment of separate regulators. Second, I show how the interplay of different international organizations, both institutions and firms, accounts for key differences in the form of regulatory reform, as well as for some privatization outcomes. Third, this chapter shows how countries retain distinct, national responses to global and European pressures for reform, as shown through their patterns of privatization and variation in the implementation and effectiveness of the new separate regulators. Also in evidence are political commitments to particular styles of governance, which includes variation within a "Nordic culture of governance."

These four upper-income countries are most similar in that they are all small and members of the OECD. All have become members of the EU (although Finland and Sweden are late joiners), and all are highly integrated into the international market. They are also unique in their approach to concerns for the domestic welfare state and other redistributive policies. Furthermore, some of the regulators and key companies in all four countries have been highly involved in other, middle-income countries, thus providing an opportunity to trace interdependent decision making and policy learning across countries.

THEMES IN TELECOMMUNICATIONS REFORM

Shifts Toward Telecommunications Liberalization in Northern Europe

Sweden and Denmark started to liberalize their telecommunications markets as early as 1995, and the Netherlands followed suit soon thereafter. According to interviews with a Dutch regulator, "we wanted to be progressive – and there was a policy competition, a noble rivalry among regulators."[2]

[2] Interview with Dutch regulator at OPTA, March 2004.

In Northern Europe, some of the main market trends include fixed-to-mobile substitution and an increased number of people owning only mobile phones. Broadband has been extended, and there is a high degree of competition in most market segments. The national regulatory agencies are mostly seen to be independent and able to regulate effectively, although each country has had its own share of questions about national regulatory authority (NRA) decisions and other regulatory approaches.

Explaining Key Similarities in Liberal Telecom Reform

All four countries are highly competitive market economies and are well-regarded as early liberalizers in the EU and OECD. Also, all countries are members of the World Trade Organization (WTO), in addition holding membership in other European networks of regulators and telecom associations. Global diffusion pressures through international organizations explain overall direction of reform and the timing of establishing new separate regulators.

Diffusion Through Information Networks

All four countries participated in information networks, including the International Telecommunications Union (ITU) and the OECD peer-reviewed processes of regulatory reform. The idea of promoting competitive markets through liberalization and deregulation spread throughout most members of the OECD, although it is clear that each of the countries in this book proceeded with its own policies of regulatory reform and technological transformation.

Diffusion Through Harmonization Networks

All four countries are members of the WTO and made commitments to opening their telecommunications markets to full market access and national treatment of operators, and all adopted the WTO Reference Paper of the Basic Agreement on Telecommunications in 1997. Also, all four countries adopted the EU regulations for telecoms, including the 1998 Liberalization requirements, and they implemented the Framework on Electronic Communications in 2002 and 2009. These pressures definitely explain some of the patterns of reform, but allow considerable leeway for countries' actual implementation of reforms.

Diffusion Through Networks of Regulators

Each of the four countries has participated in the Independent Regulators Group (IRG), the European Regulators Group (ERG), and, subsequently, the Body of European Regulators for Electronic Communications (BEREC). The Netherlands held the presidency of the ERG and IRG for many years, and all regulators have met regularly and exchanged views on best practices, European directives and regulations, and other pressing issues.

Diffusion Through Networks of Firms

Each of the four countries has an incumbent telecommunications operator that has embarked on international expansion over the past thirty years. As outlined later, specific mergers and acquisitions and particular investments and operations in other countries vary, but all four countries have had firms with significant international activity during the time of great global market expansion.

EXPLAINING KEY DIFFERENCES IN LIBERAL REFORM: INTERNATIONAL ORGANIZATIONS AND ENDURING NATIONAL PATTERNS

Privatization

These four countries of northern Europe also diverge in terms of their privatization of incumbents. Only Denmark fully privatized its dominant public telecommunications operator, TeleDanmark. The other three countries have partially privatized their telecom firms, Telia (Sweden), KPN (Netherlands), and Sonera (Finland). These firms are well-regarded as competitive in their home markets, as well as in the general Baltic and northern region, and even in Eastern Europe. State ownership does not seem to be a barrier to competitiveness, but rather acts as a stabilizing force for competition and economic growth, counter to some of the neoliberal advice given to transitional and developing countries.

Separate Regulator

The four northern countries diverge in their practice of where the separate regulator is housed. Although the regulators are all recognized to be independent, only the Netherlands has an independent regulator separate from the government policy-maker. Denmark, Finland, and Sweden's regulators are located within ministries, although with separate budget items. This practice is quite different from the advice of some of the proponents of new institutional economics, who argue in favor of separating the regulator from both the incumbent operator and government ministry. And, whereas in developing or transitional countries this might not be a policy option, the northern European countries seem quite capable of enforcing regulatory decisions and maintaining the competitiveness of the economy. This suggests a different, perhaps "Nordic" model of regulatory agencies.

COUNTRY-SPECIFIC REGULATORY REFORM

Denmark: "The Best and Cheapest Telecom Services – Through Real Competition"

Denmark led the way in terms of both liberalization and privatization, as well as in developing a proactive regulator. As early as 1995, the research ministry declared its policy goals of providing "the best and the cheapest – through real competition." Others have presented excellent overviews of earlier phases in Denmark's telecom policy developments (Henten and Wulff 1996; Melody 2002). Compared with the other Nordic countries in this chapter, Denmark was one of the most liberal nations, yet it also pursued a different path with its government's commitment to pursuing policy goals. In terms of interacting with international organizations,

Denmark is a member of all of the major international organizations under study (OECD, WTO, EU) and was an early member of the EU. Yet, Denmark does not just "receive" policies from the EU without question. Denmark showed its own political path and concerns when voting on the Maastricht Treaty in the early 1990s, and many politicians within Denmark remain skeptical of some EU decisions.

Market Developments

As of 2009, Denmark had a population of 5.5 million and a gross domestic product (GDP) of US$308.9 billion, with a GDP per capita of US$56,100 (Central Intelligence Agency [CIA], 2005–2011, in World Factbook for 2010). The Danish krona trades at around 5.6 to US$1 as of 2010.

According to the EU, increasing numbers of Danes are using bundled packages. Triple-play packages of internet, telephony (fixed or mobile), and television are increasingly popular (European Commission 2010b, the Digital Scorecard 2010, Denmark, p. 2). Denmark has set an action plan for developing digital infrastructure buildout to reach a substantial percentage of the population at a fast speed by 2020. Denmark already has one of the highest broadband penetrations in the EU (38.8 percent of the population), through both fixed-line and mobile providers (European Commission 2010b). Privatized electric utility companies have continued to invest in the rollout of fiber to the home (FTTH) networks (European Commission 2010b, p. 3).

The mobile telephony market is characterized by strong retail competition among four providers, with some increase in mobile broadband. Mobile penetration in Denmark rose to 136 percent in 2010, well above the EU average of 124.2 percent. The incumbent's mobile subsidiary for voice services was 40.5 percent in terms of subscribers, and the main competitor's market share was 28 percent (NITA Statistics). The number of fixed telephony subscribers (PTSN lines) continued to decrease in Denmark to 2 million subscribers (78.7 percent), although there was growth in the area of Internet Protocol (IP) telephony.

Firms

The cross-cutting ownership patterns of incumbents and alternative providers can be found in all of the countries in the region, particularly in Denmark, Finland, Norway, and Sweden, although several of these firms have branched out to other regions, including Central Europe.

TDC[3] was known as TeleDanmark until December 2000, and continues to be the country's dominant provider of fixed line, broadband, and wireless telephony. TDC is privately owned by a group of equity groups, as well as by the Danish pension fund ATP, private investors, and TDC employees.

Telia Denmark[4] (including Call Me and DLG) is a subsidiary of the Swedish telecoms group Telia-Sonera, which entered the Danish telecommunications market in 1995 as an alternate fixed-line operator. Telia has its own fiber-optic cable network. In 2004, Telia purchased and took over Orange Denmark's wireless and wireline businesses.

Telenor Denmark (Tele2, Sonofon, and Cybercity)

Swedish telecommunications group Tele2 started services in Denmark in 1996, after the liberalization reform that opened competition in the market. The Swedish group opted to divest its holdings in Denmark and sold its shares to the Norwegian incumbent Telenor,[5] whose existing Danish operations included Sonofon and Cybercity. This sale proceeded in 2007, and the merged company became known under the common brand of Telenor Denmark.

In 1996, Denmark was one of the earliest countries in Europe to liberalize multiple segments of its telecommunications markets, including local, long-distance, and international telephony, wireless markets, and broadband.

All operators, fixed or wireless, must allow their networks and services to be interconnected with other players that request

[3] http://www.tdc.dk
[4] http://www.telia.dk
[5] http://telenor.dk

access. Any firm with significant market power (SMP); especially the incumbent TDC needs to allow rivals to offer their services over its own infrastructure. Some existing operators have complained that the system is too "light-handed" (International Telecommunications Union [ITU] 2002).

In 1998, Telia Denmark and Orange launched global system for communication (GSM) networks. Denmark introduced number portability in mobile service very early, in 2001, and awarded third-generation (3G) licenses that same year to TDC Mobil, Telia, Orange, and Hi3G. The four main wireless providers as of 2010 include TDC, Telenor Denmark, Telia Denmark, and Hi3G (European Commission 2010a).

The incumbent is TeleDanmark, now known as TDC, and it provides fixed, wireless, and broadband packages of services. The fixed-line market in Denmark was opened right after market liberalization in 1996, and Tele2 and Telia Denmark launched services that year. Almost ten years later, Telenor of Norway bought the Danish operations of Swedish Tele2 Group and merged them with its own Sonofon, renaming both entities Telenor Denmark (European Commission 2010a).

TDC continues to hold about 45 percent of the market for wireless subscribers, followed by Telenor Denmark (28 percent), Telia Denmark (20.7 percent), and Hi3G Access Denmark (8.6 percent) (European Commission 2010b).

Main Regulatory Developments

A number of acts and executive orders govern the telecom sector in Denmark (for a full list, see http://en.itst.dk/law-material). The National IT and Telecommunications Agency (Telesyrelsen or National IT and Telecommunications Agency [NITA]) was the main regulator for telecommunications, and was a division of the Ministry of Science, Technology, and Innovation (MTSI). This division was established in 2002, when the National Telecommunications Agency was merged with the Danish State Information Service. This agency also worked with the Danish Competition Agency (DCA), which is an autonomous entity under the Ministry of Economic and Business Affairs that promotes competition through the Consolidated Act on Competitive Conditions and Consumer Interests in the Telecommunications Market (2005/7) (European Commission 2010a). The NITA was disbanded this past year, and its functions were delegated to two different ministries, the Danish Business Authority and the Danish Agency for Digitization.[6]

In 2010, the Danish NRA (IT-og Telestyrelsen [NITA]), made seven rulings, of which six were upheld. NITA's independence was set out in national legislation, and, according to the EU Digital Scorecard, most operators considered it to have carried out its tasks appropriately (European Commission 2010b, Denmark, p. 3). This number of rulings is much lower than in 2009, when the Telecommunications Complaint Board made eighteen rulings, of which sixteen upheld NITA's decisions (European Commission 2009, Denmark, p. 145).

The NITA imposed an asymmetric mobile termination rate on mobile operators so that the new 3G provider might enter into competition with the three other mobile network operators. This rate was to be leveled after one year.

According to the EU, alternative operators are concerned about the incumbent's dominance in the fixed market, which has been rather stable for the past ten years (European Commission 2010b, Denmark, p. 7). There also were concerns about mandatory membership in and payment to local cable TV associations as a barrier to entry for new companies, as well as a way to prevent some rollout and adoption of fiber and other technologies. NITA led a working group consisting of five ministries, the Danish Competition Authority, and local government in Denmark to investigate this market dominance (European Commission 2009, Denmark, p. 148).

The Danish telecom market used to be divided into regional areas serviced by regional telecom operators with exclusive rights, and a state operator that managed interregional and international communications, also with exclusive rights. In 1990, Tele Danmark was created as a holding company to take over and integrate those

[6] Please refer to http://en.itst.dk/; accessed 09-12-2012

regional operators, a task completed in 1996. The goal of the Danish government was to strengthen the Danish market, then liberalize the national and international market. Danish policies changed course after 1996, with priorities shifting from industrial policy to one of infrastructure and market development. Some analysts claim this action to be inspired by similar statements about an Information Society from the European Commission and countries such as the United States.

The overall goal for the Danish regulatory framework was to provide conditions for the creation of real competition, as phrased in the discourse of Danish telecom policy, as it was not enough to rely on the possibilities of liberalization and privatization. A related goal was to ensure universal service at affordable prices for users and the protection of user's rights. These goals emerged particularly after 1996, after the privatization of the Danish telecom operator and introduction of liberalization into the market.

Denmark fully liberalized its telecom markets in 1996, well before the EU deadline of January 1998, and fully privatized the formerly state-owned incumbent in 1995, now known as TDC (TeleDanmark). The last remaining shares were sold to Ameritech and later taken over by SBC, which retained 42 percent ownership. The Danish state retained some state ownership in telecoms through a minority share (10.2 percent) in Orange Denmark, the mobile telecommunications firm also owned by France Télécom, which is held by the state railway agency, Banestyrelsen.

During 2000, more than forty-five operators were active in the market for fixed-line voice telephony, which decreased to thirty in August 2003. As of 2003, there were four licensed GSM network operators and an additional sixteen mobile service providers. Overall investment in telecoms has decreased, partially due to the crisis in the telecom sector in general.

The regulatory authority in charge of sector-specific telecommunications regulation was the NITA, which coordinated its positions with the Danish Competition Authority when required. The NITA was a separate and independent agency affiliated with the Ministry for Science, Technology, and Innovation. The first national regulatory authority, the National Telecommunications Agency, was established in 1991, during the process of liberalizing the telecom market and preparing TeleDanmark for privatization. Previously, a telecom regulatory institution had been established in 1919, to regulate the privately owned regional companies, which existed until the mid-1980s, but which had expertise only in technical matters, as opposed to more broad policy initiatives. In 1997, Parliament passed legislation to strengthen the telecom regulator and to highlight its independent status, which was subsequently repealed and reformulated under the 2002 telecommunications act, without any change in independence or authority.

Some analysts argue that regulatory intervention in Denmark has played a critical role in generating a competitive telecom market environment, and that the fine performance on prices and services to consumers is driven more by the regulator than by actual competition itself (Henten 2004). An ITU survey reveals that a "cooperative spirit" exists between the regulatory authority and the operators in Denmark in the form of industry agreements (self-regulation) and topical seminars on interconnection, best practices, and other issues, sponsored by the regulator (ITU 2002).

Although Denmark joined the EU in 1973, it has opted out of some elements of the Maastricht Treaty, including European Economic and Monetary Union (EMU), European Defense Cooperation, and some other issues including justice and home affairs. As Denmark chose not to participate in EMU, it has not adopted the Euro as a currency, although it remains committed to pursuing the European single market in other areas. Denmark also participates in other international organizations, including the WTO, the ITU, the OECD, the North Atlantic Treaty Organization (NATO), the European Conference of Postal and Telecommunications Administration (CEPT), and other many other organizations.

The Danish electorate rejected the EMU in 2000, in a closely run ballot, as voters feared a loss of political independence and national sovereignty. The Danish currency is pegged to the Euro, but there has been no major movement to shift to the Euro. In this way, as in telecommunications, Denmark continues to fly its own colors of red and white, even while being a member of the EU.

Finland: "Nordic Values of Equity and Solidarity"

In Helsinki, it is possible to use a Nokia cellphone to purchase soft drinks from a vending machine, in addition to calling anywhere in the world. Finland has shifted its economy from natural resources, forestry, and industrial production to become one of the world leaders in the new economy, particularly in the production of information-communications technology and services. Finland is among a handful of countries leading the world in the production of cellular mobile handsets and innovations in services.

Main Market Developments

The Finnish market for electronic communications is very innovative, particularly in the realm of mobile and broadband communication. Some of the main trends include increased fixed-to-mobile substitution, including that of mobile broadband. Finland reached the highest EU mobile broadband penetration in 2009 (European Commission 2009, Finland, p. 167). Prices for mobile consumers are low, and availability of services is high. In the fixed-line market, rates are relatively high and revenues are low. There is a high degree of competition, particularly in mobile services, and the NRA is considered to be independent and effective.

Finland continues to lead in broadband development, and was the first country to recognize access to broadband as a universal legal right. As of 2010, all Finns are entitled to a 1 megabit per second (Mbit/s) broadband connection. In October 2009, Finland's Ministry of Transport and Communications had announced that the country's Communications Market Act had been amended to include internet access of 1 Mbit/s as part of the universal service obligations and as a legal right, and that the amendment would become effective in the summer of 2010.

Suvi Lindén, Finland's Minister of Communications welcomed the new law: "From now on, a reasonably priced broadband connection will be everyone's basic right in Finland. This is absolutely one of the government's most significant achievements in regional policy and I am proud of it," she said (FICORA 2010–12).

Telia-Sonera Finland is now the major telecommunications operator in the country, offering digital subscriber line (DSL) services. The operator has also been offering asymmetric DSL (ADSL) services through its brand Auria. In addition to fixed broadband, Telia-Sonera offers mobile broadband and telephony services.

The other two large alternative operators with their own networks are Elisa and DNA, offering fixed and mobile services. In addition to these, around twenty-five regional telecom operators formed the Finnet group, with each of these companies owning a fixed network in its respective region. The largest mobile operators with their own networks are DNA, Elisa, and Telia-Sonera (European Commission 2009, Finland).

A particular feature of the broadband market is the increase in the number of mobile broadband subscribers, coupled with a decline in the number of fixed broadband subscribers. The Economist Intelligence Unit's annual rankings put Finland among the world's leading countries for using information and communications technologies (ICT) for economic and social benefit. Finland is ranked fourth in the 2011 assessment, up from tenth in 2009 (EIU, Economist Intelligence Unit 1999–2010, country reports for 2011).

"Finland has worked hard to develop an equitable and inclusive information society. We were the first country in the world to ensure – by legislation – that all our citizens have the opportunity to use digital services – irrespective of their place of residence, whether in the city or the countryside, or the level of their income," said President Tarja Halonen of Finland. "Already now, a good and reasonably priced Internet connection is everyone's right in Finland," she added (see http://www.itu.int/net/itunews/issues/2011/04/10.aspx).

The competitive environment in Finland has been intense but stable, with four main market players, three with their own mobile, trunk, and access networks and the fourth (an association of local incumbents) providing fixed-line telephony. This association established a new network operator.

Mobile phones are plentiful in Finland, and more than 86 percent of the total volume of calls originate in mobile networks, with a penetration rate of 150 percent (European Commission 2010b, Finland). The mobile market has been growing rapidly, with an increase in subscribers (8.1 million in 2010) and traffic volumes, particularly in data services.

Finland has a unique service structure, with a very high number of small, local fixed incumbents in their traditional operating areas enjoying high market share. In terms of all calls by traffic volume, the incumbents' market share stood at 96 percent in December 2009 (European Commission 2010b, Finland).

Main Regulatory Development

Finland opened its markets to full competition in 1994, well before most other countries in the OECD. Deregulation was a priority in an economy that previously was closed and had significant restrictions on market entry. Finland has a large, segmented market of local operators acting within local areas. In 2003, Finland had more than seventy SMP operators in the communications markets, which posed significant regulatory challenges in how to define relevant geographic markets, how to regulate local operators of vastly different shapes and sizes, and how to regulate the specific terms of interconnection and universal access provisions (FICORA 2010–12). Although competition was introduced early, the regulator has acknowledged the challenges of bottleneck resources, which have posed problems in the Finnish market. Finland has applied both competition law and sector-specific law to grapple with these problems of bottleneck resources, as well as to enhance the overall competitiveness of its market.

Finland was a leader in implementing the new European framework for electronic communications with the passage of the Communications Market Act of July 25, 2003. Like some other Scandinavian countries, Finland characterizes its own regulatory regime as "light," in that it emphasizes the importance of market forces and does not, for example, impose ex ante price regulation.

The NRA, the Finnish Communications Regulatory Authority (the Viestintävirasto Kommunikationsverket or FICORA), has the legal authority to carry out tasks of market regulation and consumer protection. A EU report on the implementation of the common regulatory framework shows that "according to market players, FICORA is considered as an efficient and impartial regulator" (European Commission 2009, Finland p. 168; European Commission 2010b, Finland). The policy-maker in Finland is the Ministry of Transport and Communications.

FICORA has set up a website (www.viestintävirasto.fi) for Finnish consumers to check which geographic areas have been assigned a universal service operator for the provision of broadband subscriptions, which may be implemented via fixed or wireless technology (http://www.itu.int/net/itunews/issues/2010/06/34.aspx).

The key players in regulation and competition of telecommunications in Finland are FICORA, which regulates the electronic communications sector, and the Finnish Competition Authority (FCA).

Finland's commitment to the WTO Basic Agreement on Telecommunications Services includes market access and national treatment for all services. Finland adopted the WTO Reference Paper.

The Netherlands

Main Market Developments

As of 2009, the Netherlands had a population of 16.5 million, a GDP of US$796 billion, and a GDP per capita of US$48,200 (CIA 2005–2011, in World Factbook for 2009). The Netherlands is a member of the EU and the Eurozone. Although a key member of the Eurozone, Dutch voters did reject the proposed EU Constitution in June 2005, in a show of Euro-skepticism.

Some recent statistics from the market for telecommunications in the Netherlands show that, like other countries, the dominant form of telecommunications is wireless, and the number of households with fixed telephone lines is decreasing. The total number of wireless subscribers in 2010 was 19.39 million, with a market penetration of 116 percent. Broadband subscribers totaled 6 million, with a market penetration of

85.6 percent. Fixed-line subscribers numbered 7.26 million households, representing 97 percent, but this figure was much lower for individuals (European Commission 2010b, the Netherlands).

The electronic communications market in the Netherlands as of 2009 is characterized by widespread broadband access, with choice among providers for affordable prices and increasing speeds (European Commission 2009, the Netherlands, p. 299).

More than 3.7 million subscribers use either double-play or triple-play services that include at least fixed voice telephony (OPTA). The number of fixed-line telephony subscribers dropped, as did the volume of calls. The incumbent remains the main provider of fixed telephony services (70 percent of subscribers).

The Netherlands has the highest broadband penetration in Europe, with 38.9 percent as of January 2011, much higher than the EU average of 26.6 percent (European Commission 2010b, the Netherlands, p. 1). Both cable and DSL networks are active, and the incumbent is rolling out fiber to the home. Mobile penetration as of 2010 was around 116 percent, with higher traffic volumes.

Major players in the Dutch telecommunications market include some of the "usual suspects" in other European networks. KPN is the dominant provider of bundled services, and other major players include T-Mobile Netherlands (owned by Deutsche Telekom, and purchased the shares of France Télécom's Orange), Tele2 NL (owned by the Tele2 group in Sweden), and Vodafone Netherlands (owned by Vodafone, with shares from Great Britain). In terms of broadband, UPC Netherlands is the main cable company (wholly owned by UPC Broadband, which is majority-owned by Liberty Global). Another cable company is Zesko Holding (Ziggo), owned by private equity firms (European Commission 2010a).

The number of traditional public switched traditional network (PSTN) lines decreased throughout 2010, along with the volume of fixed-line telephony. The incumbent remains the main provider of direct access to fixed-telephony services (65 percent of all subscribers).

The Netherlands introduced liberal market-oriented reforms slowly over the 1990s, sometimes leading and sometimes lagging behind other European countries, especially Denmark. Policy-makers in the Netherlands corporatized KPN, the flagship telecom operator, in 1989, and, as of 1993, they had liberalized the markets for data transport and the sale of leased lines. In 1994, voice markets were liberalized, and 30 percent of shares of KPN were sold to private investors. The Netherlands slowly introduced competition in GSM licenses, satellites, cable networks, fixed-line telephony, and finally, all voice by 1997. Some competition began to emerge as early as the reforms in 1993, but, for the most part, competition was only introduced later, especially in the late 1990s (de Bijl and Peitz 2000).

The Dutch regulatory agency is the Independent Post and Telecommunications Authority (Onafhankelijke Post en Telecommunicatie Autoriteit, OPTA),[7] which was established in 1997 (Mansell, Davies, and Hulsink 1996). The OPTA is responsible for implementing the Telecommunications and Postal Acts in the Netherlands, and one of the chairmen of OPTA, Jens Arnbak, has played a key international role, holding chairmanships of both the IRG and the ERG. The Ministry responsible for telecommunications shifted in 2002 from the Directorate General for Telecommunications and Post to the Ministry of Economic Affairs.

The OPTA determines which operators hold significant market power (SMP). This concept has changed over the past ten years, as some initial rigidities have been loosened, and it no longer applies simply to those operators with more than a 25 percent share of the market. Those operators with SMP must provide cost-oriented interconnection tariffs, to ensure competitive access to bottleneck facilities and to provide choices for end users. Other scholars have documented more micro-level processes of regulatory shifts, especially in the relationship between liberalization and re-regulation of interconnection policies and terminal type-approval (Levi-Faur 1999).

The Dutch looked to the examples of how Oftel, the British regulator, was tough on the monopolist British Telecom, as it was

[7] For the most recent information, please consult http://www.opta.nl.

an early example. Also, the Dutch regulators found it easier to understand the English language. While the Danes and the Italians had early regulators, it was "more difficult" for Dutch policy-makers to read the decisions and interpret how to apply the principles in the Dutch market.[8]

Main Regulatory Developments

Some of the legislation for the Dutch market for telecommunications and electronic communications includes the Telecommunications Act of 2004, designed to bring into effect the five EU directives on electronic communication.

The Dutch regulatory authority, OPTA, has experienced some conflicts with the Dutch Court in recent years. In 2009, several important market decisions were annulled by the business court, and around half of all OPTA decisions have been challenged in the Court since 2009. According to the EU Digital Scoreboard, "this has led to regulatory uncertainty, which has been reflected in both the operators' business decisions as in the market in general" (European Commission 2010b, the Netherlands, p. 1). The NRA in some cases is required to amend its decisions, and it also needs to restart the market analysis procedure, including public consultation procedures, market definition procedures, identification of SMP undertaking, and the imposition of remedies (European Commission 2009, the Netherlands).

Sweden

Sweden had a population of 9.3 million, a GDP of US$403 billion, and a GDP per capita of US$43,400 as of 2009 (CIA 2005–2011, in World Factbook 2010, Sweden). Although Sweden joined the EU in 1995, it is not a member of the Eurozone and retains its own currency, the Swedish krona (crown). In the referendum of 2003, Swedish voters decidedly rejected membership in the unified currency organization.

[8] Interview with Dutch policy-makers, 2004.

Sweden is one of the most advanced telecommunications sectors in the world. Fixed-line subscribers had a penetration rate of 64 percent in 2003, whereas mobile penetration was more than 95 percent in the same year (EIU, Economist Intelligence Union 1999–2010, Country Profile for Sweden 2005). Similar to other European countries, mobile subscriptions skyrocketed in the 1990s, and now most citizens have phones. The Swedish telecommunications market was opened to liberalization in 1993, well in advance of other European countries on the continent. In 2002, the Swedish and Finnish partly state-owned incumbents merged into one firm, Telia-Sonera. Although Sweden has more than forty telecom operators, Telia-Sonera remains dominant in many market segments. Alternatives to the long-distance infrastructure are provided by a number of competitive firms.

Unlike other European countries, Sweden did not have an auction for 3G licenses in mobile telephony; rather, Sweden chose to award contracts on the basis of the speed and quality of infrastructure, and, in 2000, Sweden issued four contracts to Tele2, the mobile branch of the telecom firm Netcom; Vodafone (UK); Orange Sweden (joint venture including France Télécom); and Hi3G. The overall goal of introducing these 3G licenses was to provide universal mobile access to Swedish citizens by 2003, but these goals were not realized. Orange withdrew in 2002, and its shares were taken over by Telia-Sonera and Tele2. The build-out and launch was delayed for several years (European Commission 2009, Sweden).

Sweden established its separate telecom regulator, the National Post and Telecommunications Agency, in 1992, around the time of the first liberalization efforts in the Swedish telecom market. The regulator is known to be independent, yet it reports to the Ministry.

International influence in Sweden includes the EU, particularly since its accession in 1995. Although Sweden began its telecom liberalization efforts prior to joining the EU, it has since adopted the main principles of the EU package on telecom reforms in 1998, as well as the 2002 framework on Electronic Communications, with amendments in 2009 and beyond (European Commission 2010b, Sweden).

Firms

Major market players include Telia-Sonera Sweden, the dominant incumbent. The Swedish government is the largest shareholder in Telia-Sonera, with 37.3 percent of shares. The Finnish government holds 13.7 percent of shares, with the rest distributed among other shareholders. Telia-Sonera is the country's main provider of fixed-line voice services, as well as broadband internet access and IP telephony. Telenor Sweden was formerly Vodafone Sweden. Telenor Sweden sells to mobile, fixed-line, and broadband customers in residential and business market segments. Telenor Sweden is wholly owned by Telenor of Norway, which in turn is owned by the Norwegian state (53 percent) and other shareholders. In terms of broadband, some of the main providers are Hi3G Access Sweden and the main cable provider, Com Hem (including UPC Sweden) (European Commission 2010a).

Main Regulatory Developments

Sweden liberalized local telephony, domestic long-distance telephony, and international telephony in January 1993, well ahead of many other European countries. This was around the same time that the first wireless operators began service in Sweden (Comvik, now part of Tele2, Telia-Sonera, and Telenor [formerly Vodafone]). The Electronic Communications Act (2003) replaced the previous Telecommunications Act (SFS 1993: 957) and the Radiocommunications Act (SFS 1993: 599).

The systematic appeals of NRA decisions have thwarted many elements of effective market regulation in Sweden. Legislation requires that appeals take six months, but most operators consider that the time between filing an appeal to decision by the Court remains too long (European Commission 2010b, Sweden, p. 1). The Swedish government has launched a Digital Agenda for Sweden that is inspired by the Digital Agenda for Europe (DAE).[9]

[9] For further information, please consult http://www.sweden.gov.se/sb/d/2025/a/181914 (accessed September 12, 2012).

In August 2009, the government introduced an amendment to the competition law to help mitigate the charges that public actors were receiving an unfair advantage over private actors in the provision of services.

CONCLUSION

The northern European countries, although advanced liberal reformers that belong to many of the same international institutions, display great differences in liberalization, privatization, and the establishment of separate regulators, both among the four countries in this study and between other countries of the OECD and EU. Each country chose different paths to establishing separate regulators and privatizing incumbents. Denmark, for example, is the only one to privatize the main state-owned incumbent entirely. Finland and Sweden still retain majority state ownership of the joint venture, Telia-Sonera, and KPN of the Netherlands has state minority shares. Although each country is highly ranked in terms of competitiveness, three countries – Denmark, Finland, and Sweden – have national telecommunications agencies that are separate from the incumbent, but are still located within a ministry. This does not fit with the general set of liberal policy norms, but it appears that the regulatory agency is able to make decisions and promote an overall liberal and competitive environment. The Netherlands, however, has a regulatory agency separate from the dominant incumbent and the ministry, and it is located in the Hague.

These findings suggest that international policy diffusion and the emergence of new actors play out differently among competitive Nordic countries than in other market economies in Europe, and that the mechanisms, too, might be different. The findings also suggest the continued importance of national characteristics, although these may be broadening as cross-ownership of firms may provide a need for cross-regulator cooperation.

CHAPTER 6

Explaining Change in a Globalized World

International Organizations and the Emergence of Networks and Norms

Since 1995, many countries have liberalized their telecom sectors within a condensed timeframe, while, at the same time, state-level decision-makers have enacted liberal regulatory reform in telecommunications in a context of globalization and Europeanization. This book has demonstrated that international organizations, not national governments, market forces, or international norms, are the primary drivers of policy convergence in the important area of telecommunications and the broader field of electronic communications. International organizations play three critical roles in the diffusion of domestic institutional innovations: (1) they create and shape preferences for reform, (2) they provide forums for expert discussions, and (3) they provide forums for the emergence of policy standards. Yet, international organizations and international policy convergence leave room for substantial variation among national cases.

This book has shown the degree to which liberal ideology in the approach of liberalization and introduction of competition has spread in institutions around the world, particularly through the diffusion channels of organizations dedicated to the spread of free trade (World Trade Organization [WTO], European Union [EU]), as well as organizations dedicated to liberal market principles in general (Organization for Economic Cooperation and Development [OECD]). Competition is seen as a valuable method of unleashing the market forces that can bring prosperity to citizens and consumers by allowing for the provision of more services and goods at reasonable prices.

If liberal ideology and the promise of prosperity and great gains required the introduction of actual competition, governments needed to signal to markets that there was indeed opportunity to participate and gain, even under conditions in which the incumbents had significant market power. With the leadership and adoption of such ideas by key countries, such as the United States and the United Kingdom, as well as substantial pressures in the form of the General Agreement on Trade in Services (GATS) Negotiation and the Telecommunications Agreement of 1996, the norm of separating a regulatory office from the operation of the telecommunications firm became entrenched. Some developing countries, especially Brazil and Venezuela, played key roles in advancing the overall agenda of telecommunications as a trade in services and agreed to create a separate regulatory structure.

What has not spread is the norm of privatization. Despite much liberal rhetoric about the importance of securing transparent property rights and rolling back the role of the state, many of the largest firms in telecommunications are owned by large governments (e.g., Deutsche Telekom, Telefonica). The European landscape of electronic communications is dominated by state-owned players. Although most countries indeed introduced some form of private sector participation in the incumbent and in the market, wide variation exists across countries in terms of the particular form and function of state ownership.

In the wake of the world financial crisis of 2008, the European financial crisis of 2010–11, and the global Occupy Movement, the liberal model of market economies and regulations have come into question. The predominant liberal economic paradigm of liberalization, privatization, and deregulation has accompanied the development of further income inequalities globally. What began in the post-war years in terms of embedded liberalism and the expansion of markets in free trade led to an ideological movement to roll back the state in terms of power in the economy, and to shift the role of government in the economy. In light of government bailouts and the nationalization of large firms, there are more calls for consumer protection, increased regulation, and perhaps more control over the behavior of free markets.

There is no question that the spread of markets, technology, and liberal government regulation in telecommunications has led to great prosperity in terms of lower prices and greater availability of services to citizens. Mobile phones, in particular, have become so widespread that most people around the world have some access to communications technology and the internet, and this has led to the spread of information, knowledge, and prosperity to large numbers of people. And yet, technology and liberalization have not delivered on the promises to deliver prosperity to all – structural inequalities continue to worsen in terms of income, as well as of access to further prosperity.

One of the big lessons is that deregulation does not always work. Government and the state are still important in restraining the behavior of large market participants and in ensuring the provision of public services to citizens. Although the market can bring great benefits and opportunities, there is no guarantee that Adam Smith's "invisible hand" will work as it should. Even card-carrying liberal economists like Paul Krugman, Simon Johnson (Johnson and Kwak 2011), and Joseph Stiglitz (Stiglitz 2010) have lambasted the concentration of market power in Wall Street and other large conglomerates. The issue of "too big to fail" applies to large banks, and also could be applied to large telecommunications firms.

This book has shown a great deal of convergence in terms of the concentration of power in incumbent providers of telecommunications and electronic communications services. Although there has been no global consensus about privatization, there has also been no global consensus about how competition can be maintained effectively. For example, even in the United States, arguably one of the most liberal market economies, the concentration of power among incumbent monopolists like Verizon and Comcast has shown that the U.S. Department of Justice and competition authorities have failed to maintain competitive conditions for market entrants.

I argue that state decision-makers learn from each other and through the auspices of international organizations while crafting packages of regulatory reform. Yet, despite some similarities in liberal reform, both international and domestic factors continue to explain important national-level differences. Such factors are visible in how countries privatize their operators, establish separate regulators, and develop new regulatory frameworks.

Overall, the book reveals that, to understand the phenomenon of telecom reform, it is crucial to consider how decision-makers evaluated their policy environment and used examples from other countries' behavior. International organizations played a critical role in the timing and design of separate regulatory agencies for telecommunications. In an environment of high information asymmetry, dynamism, and uncertainty, and with the emergence of an ideological consensus about the appropriateness of a separate regulatory agency, countries learned from other country examples through networks of international organizations.

Yet this dynamic does not apply to the liberalization of telecom markets or the privatization of the state-owned telecom operator, which reveals some of the scope conditions for diffusion arguments. I found that global market forces better explained the timing and extent of liberalization, and that domestic political and economic groupings, particularly state priorities, determined a country's decision to privatize the main telecom operator. In privatization, one of the key factors was the absence of international ideological consensus that private ownership, or at least privatization, was the best way to introduce changes to the state-owned telecom operator.

There are several reasons why privatization can be viewed as fundamentally different from establishing a separate regulator. One is that there is no clear ideological consensus among powerful actors, both internationally and nationally, that privatization of the incumbent is necessary. In establishing separate regulators, it seems clear that an ideological consensus that having a separate regulator has emerged and is reinforced by key powerful countries (United States, United Kingdom) and legitimated by international organizations (WTO, OECD, EU).

Many scholars and practitioners have claimed that the goal of telecommunications regulatory policy is to promote the development of information societies or network societies. Policy-makers and regulators within countries and at the EU level are continuing to articulate and define these future demands, and it remains to be seen how the politics and economics of these dynamic markets will emerge. Further, although Europe is clearly set on becoming a global leader in competitive markets, at least according to the Lisbon Goals, other regions of the world continue to work on these policy initiatives as well, particularly in the context of the World Summit on the Information Society in 2003 and 2005, as well as in more recent years.[1]

Although all countries in Europe have adopted the principles of both the 1998 framework and the Framework on Electronic Communication 2002 and 2009, the mode and speed of implementation of the EU directives varies significantly across countries and across markets. In Europe, most member states experienced serious legislative difficulty at some point during the process, including the ongoing hurdles of transposing the six new directives and one decision. The transposition also requires each country to enact not only the directives themselves, but secondary legislation related to the directives, including measures for state administration, competition authorities, and more. The European Commission recently launched an inquiry against France and other major European member states for their failure to transpose the directives on electronic commerce.[2]

Some of the common problems include the lack of experience in writing and enforcing telecom regulation and legislations, as well as hurdles when encountering the legislature. Some of these regulations have not been tested anywhere, and all countries face challenges in how to regulate a dynamic sector while still providing

[1] For further information, please see http://www.itu.int/wsis/index.html (accessed September 12, 2012).

[2] Please refer to the Europa website for more current information on EU regulations, enforcement, and infringement proceedings http://ec.europa.eu/information_society/policy/ecomm/implementation_enforcement/infringement/index_en.htm (accessed September 12, 2012).

service in the public interest. The European Regulators Group (ERG) and the Body of Regulators for Electronic Communications (BEREC) were designed to accelerate and enhance the harmonization of the directives and encourage the development of a single market for telecommunications services, yet it remains unclear how and to what extent some of these visions will be realized, particularly in the varied regions of the new EU-25.

The EU and its member states continue to face the challenges of how to increase competition and provide better services at affordable prices to a pan-European market; how to accommodate trends in convergence, defined here as the technical convergence of voice, data, and media; and how to support the development of an information and network society. Yet, there has not been a demand for a sector-specific pan-European regulator on the part of national governments and certainly not of national telecom operators. Some actors in the European Commission might prefer to have a pan-European regulator, as policy-making is more tractable with only one decision-maker rather than a complex web of twenty-five regulatory authorities. Also, some incumbents might prefer to have one pan-European regulator because of the possible ease of capture – or at least of lobbying in Brussels. It takes less effort to lobby one regulator than to lobby twenty-five regulators. Yet, the winning voice seems to be that of member states, who prefer to maintain the principles of subsidiarity. A softer, more coordinated yet decentralized approach seems to be the preferred model for the newly emerging regime for electronic communications. Some argue that countries are too different, markets are too varied and complex (especially with all the new members), and the politics are too complicated to be regulated by a large government body. Others, for example in individual national parliaments and councils of ministers, may fear the possibilities of increased concentrated power in the Commission. In any case, there is very little political will to establish a pan-European super-regulator; what seems to be emerging is a softer, more decentralized regime for telecommunications regulation.

An open question remains as to the role of the European Court of Justice (ECJ) in prosecuting telecom cases – especially in those countries that do not implement the directives on electronic communications. The continuing interplay between regulators, courts, and the EU will be most interesting to observe in the coming years, particularly with the emergence of so many new actors and changes in technology. Although the ECJ has published some of its case law in telecommunications[3], there is still the challenge of constantly changing domestic legislation and judicial decisions on telecommunications within member states, a process that is not transparent and is difficult to predict. Some key participants in the telecom reform process have asked "who will judge the judges?"

To what extent do these findings reflect only conditions in Europe, and to what extent can we generalize to other regions around the world? As shown in the descriptive statistics and from the overview in Chapter 1, countries around the world share a common struggle to reap the rewards of an international economy, provide appropriate governance for their citizens, and assure access to the information economy and thus the possibility of an information society. This analysis has focused on two types of countries within Europe, middle-income countries in transition and small, high-income countries, and it has used a most-similar systems design to analyze key differences between countries. It is clear from the overview of the statistical analysis that more countries in more regions around the world also have trends and variation in telecom reform, and it is important to test more thoroughly the hypotheses and findings of this study in countries that are very different from those analyzed here.

In an expanded study, some other country clusters that could be explored are paired comparisons in different regions, also clustered by income group. Botswana and South Africa are good examples of middle- to high-income countries in Africa that have adopted a set of liberal market-oriented reforms in telecommunications, and yet display considerable variation in how these

[3] For recent case law of the European Court of Justice in the field of telecommunications 2010, please consult http://ec.europa.eu/information_society/policy/ecomm/implementation_enforcement/infringement/index_en.htm (accessed September 12, 2012).

reforms were enacted and the overall effectiveness of their regulators. The telecom regulator in Botswana, for example, is known to be effective and has been profiled in a case study by the International Telecommunications Union (ITU), as well as in other analyses of effective regulation. Both Botswana and South Africa have had an influence on other countries in the Southern Cone of Africa, and have spearheaded the formation of the Telecommunications Regulators Association of Southern Africa (TRASA). Building on some of the insights gained from this project, we might expect countries of lower income to be more susceptible to the influence of international organizations or international firms, either because of low domestic capacity for creating new regulatory regimes in telecommunications or because of possible coercion of large state actors or international organizations. Preliminary evidence reveals the importance of some key international organizations, especially the United States Agency for International Development, in the process of institutional design for telecommunications, yet there remains variation across the member states of the southern African cone. Further evidence reveals the importance of the ITU as well as the World Bank (WB) in creating these new regulatory frameworks for telecommunications. Thus, although the actors in Africa are different from the regional actors of the EU, it is still possible to find the importance of emulation and learning through the channels of international organizations and activities, and not simply agentless market processes.

Another aspect that seems to be clear is the importance of the trading community on the development of a regulatory network. Membership in these regional trade networks seems to be associated with the emergence of regulatory networks. Chapters 4 and 5 revealed the linkages among regulator networks within the EU. In other regions around the world, TRASA is closely linked to the Southern African Development Community (SADC), the Eastern Caribbean Telecommunications regulator (ECTEL) is linked with the Organization of East Caribbean States (OECS), and the Association of Regulatory and Information Communications of Eastern Africa (ARICEA) is linked with the Common Market for Eastern and Southern Africa (COMESA).

Many scholars and practitioners of telecom reform engage in normative discussions about regulatory design and the formation of independent regulatory institutions – why they should be established, what shape they should take, and where they should be located. Other scholars write profusely about regulatory reform in particular countries and discuss some of the incentives for international organizations to become involved, market forces, and other aspects of the global political economy. Yet, one important variable is left out of these narratives – global policy diffusion. None of the conventional theories can explain why so many countries liberalized their telecom sectors within such a condensed timeframe. This is a story of reform homogeneity, in that countries as widely differing as Denmark and the Maldives established separate regulators and launched liberalization plans within a short time of each other. Global policy diffusion provides one lens for considering how countries take into consideration the behavior of others when devising policy innovations, especially in the area of telecom reform. Global policy diffusion suggests a general set of variables in which countries are affected by the prior decisions of peers within certain groupings, which can be measured statistically. Also, a more structured and political version of diffusion, that of socialization through international organizations (as presented in this book), helps identify some of the key conduits through which these policies travel: through information networks, harmonization networks, and regulator networks – all examples of countries getting together in international forums and comparing notes on policy reforms.

In the end, the traditional accounts of telecom regulatory reform are not satisfactory in that they are not able to identify the specific causes, actors, or mechanisms behind this vast convergence in market reforms. Although these theories can shed light on long-term enduring structures and preferences, they have a hard time explaining radical change. The diffusion approaches that are becoming more popular in the literature provide interesting insights, but the concepts and measures do not perform well in the econometric analysis of this study of telecoms reforms. For example, identifying regional patterns of reform is helpful, but what are the characteristics of region that determine why some regions are more innovative and others are not? Furthermore, some of the broader notions of global policy diffusion, as currently constructed by the proportion of prior adoptions within a peer group identified by the analyst, are more suggestive than conclusive, especially without attention being paid to the overall specific motivations of policy-makers. Also, in this analysis, the more general measures of diffusion did not produce results that were as powerful as in other settings. This partly may be due to some conceptualization and measurement issues in the data. Yet another alternative is that diffusion is more deeply embedded than is depicted and measured in this study, as well as in other studies.

Theoretically, the combination of international, domestic, and diffusion factors in an analysis of policy innovation helps provide a more complete understanding of how the world works and how to navigate the tenuous and increasingly blurred boundary between international and domestic politics.

Telecommunications itself has radically transformed over the past twenty years, and although global policy diffusion through international organizations provides one lens for analyzing these developments, another could be a more careful analysis of shifting technological incentives. Much of the theories of regulation have been developed in a protected one-country context, particularly in the United States and Britain. As more countries begin to gain experience with competition and regulation for competition, it does not seem apparent that all will converge toward one model. Rather, countries seem to retain many important and distinct characteristics that affect how their economies are regulated. All of these questions of regulation come down to several overarching issues, most particularly, to how governments respond to changes in technologies and markets, particularly in times of great revolutions in technology.

Rather than a world increasingly "flattened" by digital convergence and technological developments, the telecommunications sector, in particular, reveals the enduring powers of monopoly structures and large governments. It is not an accident that major conglomerates in the telecoms industry have formed giant cross-border mergers and acquisitions. As some companies become overextended in some markets, often overseas, this can affect the viability of firms in the home market. For example, KPN of the Netherlands had to back out of its vast international commitments and investments in the late 1990s after suffering from revenue losses. Who pays for these losses? In many instances, private shareholders pay, but there are also costs to the consumers and citizens of the world. Governments continue to have an obligation to protect and serve the public interest by regulating companies with dominant power and ensuring that citizens have access to the information economy and the growing information society. Moreover, governments are choosing to implement these goals in different ways – by locating their regulators in ministries or not, and by creating networks of regulators to exchange information on these best practices.

In terms of policy implications, it has become clear that having a separate regulatory agency has become *de rigueur* for most countries around the world. Even some of the most heavily regulated and government-owned economies have started to spin off separate regulatory agencies. Also, although there appears to be an ideological consensus that having a regulator separate from the incumbent is necessary, and having a regulator separate from the ministry is desirable, it is not apparent why that must always be the case. The policy advice for developing and transitional countries has been to establish separate agencies, yet the Nordic countries reveal that these agencies can still be in a ministry and promote a competitive market. The policy goals seem to be not so much independence of regulators for their own sake, but achieving a balance between creating and enforcing a competitive market and maintaining and protecting the public interest. In many ways, it seems that having a regulator in a ministry might actually ensure the consistency of policy goals. Furthermore, all countries seem to be struggling with the human capital component of telecom regulation. It is difficult to find the requisite trained staff familiar not only with the arcane aspects of pricing and interconnection but also with how to create and implement competitive market policies. Regulators in advanced industrial countries share some of these common problems with their brethren in the developing world, as all face the challenges of regulating in an information age. Some of these major challenges for regulation across new technological platforms include designing effective regulations and the capacity to make and enforce regulatory decisions.

Finally, the "harmonization" of standards is not a technologically neutral or always desirable phenomenon. Many analysts, particularly economists, characterize these developments as competitive and efficient, yet these concerns overlook many of the political struggles behind the crafting of regulatory reform. In the telecommunications industry, in particular, the stakes are high, as are potential losses and gains. For example, some harmonization of standards can stem from the influence of powerful firms with lobbies in Brussels and Washington, D.C. that seek to protect and preserve their market share. Whereas incumbents were national phenomena, now they may be cross-national and global, and with interests still to protect.

Some theories of the spread of liberalization and liberalism and the Washington consensus have an accompanying normative claim that liberalization, deregulation, and privatization are inherently good. Contrary to arguments that the world is now a level playing field, it appears that, in telecom regulation at least, there are enduring structures of power and the continuing need for government regulation to ensure the free functioning of markets, without capture by vested interests. While more actors are involved in creating, adopting, and promoting telecom regulations and policies, government has not lost its influence in ensuring that its citizens have access to the information society at affordable costs.

Appendices: Figures and Tables

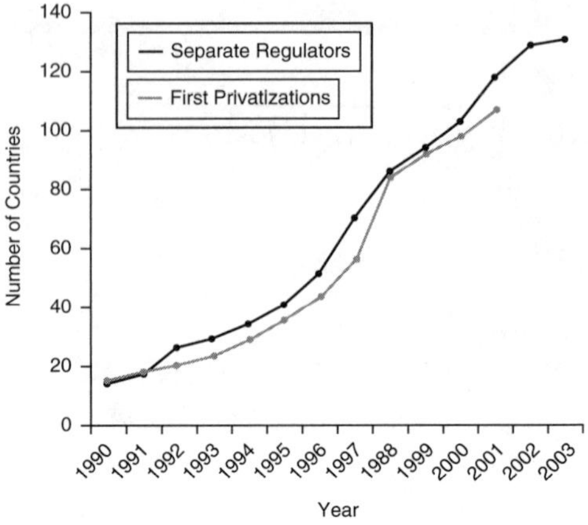

Appendix A. Total Number of Separate Regulators and First Privatizations (Source: ITU)

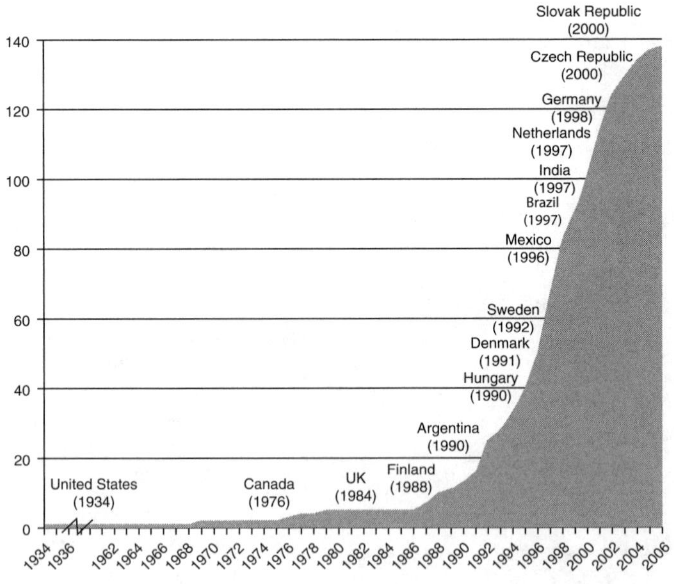

Appendix B. Cumulative Separate Regulators by 2005 (Source: ITU)

Common Forces for Change		
Marketplace Changes	**Deregulation Exported**	**Macroeconomic Trends**
• exert strong pressure to respond • apply only to dynamic sectors • apply to all countries	• exerts medium pressure to respond • applies to all sectors • applies to all countries – but some more than others	• exert weak pressure to respond • apply to all sectors • apply to all countries – but not all respond
	↓	
Global Diffusion Channels through International Organizations		
Information Networks	**Harmonization Networks**	**Regulator Networks**
• exert weak pressure to respond • utilize peer pressure through exchange of best practices • encourage information exchange • affect all countries – some more than others • apply to some sectors	• exert strong pressure to respond • utilize membership conditionality and sometimes other coercive measures • affect countries that seek membership – some more than others • apply to some sectors	• exert strong pressure to respond • utilize peer pressure to exchange best practices • use membership conditionality and coercive measures • affect countries that are in that network • apply to some sectors
• **Mechanisms:** information, emulation, mimesis, learning	• **Mechanisms:** mimesis, emulation, coercion, competition	• **Mechanisms:** best practices, mimesis, emulation, competition, coercion
	↓	
Specific National Responses		
• Pattern of state interaction in re-regulation, privatization, liberalization		

APPENDIX D. *Countries in the dataset (183 total)*

Afghanistan
Albania
Algeria
Andorra
Angola
Antigua and Barbuda
Argentina
Armenia
Australia
Austria
Azerbaijan
Bahamas
Bahrain
Bangladesh
Barbados
Belarus
Belgium
Belize
Benin
Bhutan
Bolivia
Bosnia-Hercegovina
Botswana
Brazil
Brunei Darussalam
Bulgaria
Burkina Faso
Burundi
Cambodia
Cameroon
Canada
Cape Verde
Central African Republic
Chad
Chile
China
Colombia
Comoros
Congo, Brazzaville
Congo, Kinshasa
Costa Rica
Cote d'Ivoire
Croatia
Cuba
Cyprus
Czech Republic
Denmark
Djibouti
Dominica
Dominican Republic
Ecuador
Egypt
El Salvador
Equatorial Guinea
Eritrea
Estonia
Ethiopia
Fiji
Finland
France
Gabon
Gambia
Georgia
Germany
Ghana
Greece
Grenada
Guatemala
Guinea
Guyana
Haiti
Honduras
Hungary
Iceland
India
Indonesia
Iran
Iraq
Ireland
Israel
Italy
Jamaica
Japan
Jordan
Kazakhstan
Kenya
Kiribati
Korea, DPR
Korea, Republic of
Kuwait
Kyrgistan
Lao PDR
Latvia
Lebanon
Lesotho
Liberia
Libya
Liechtenstein
Lithuania
Luxembourg
Macedonia, TFYR
Madagascar
Malawi
Malaysia
Maldives
Mali
Malta
Marshall Islands
Mauritania
Mauritius
Mexico
Micronesia
Moldova
Monaco
Mongolia
Morocco
Mozambique
Myanmar
Namibia
Nepal
Netherlands
New Zealand
Nicaragua
Niger
Nigeria
Norway
Oman
Pakistan
Panama
Papua New Guinea
Paraguay
Peru
Philippines
Poland
Portugal
Qatar
Romania
Russia
Rwanda
Sao Tome & Principe
Saudi Arabia
Senegal
Sierra Leone
Singapore
Slovak Republic
Slovenia
Solomon Islands
Somalia
South Africa
Spain
Sri Lanka
St. Lucia
St. Vincent
Sudan
Suriname
Swaziland
Sweden
Switzerland
Syria
Tajikistan
Tanzania
Thailand
Togo
Tonga
Trinidad & Tobago
Tunisia
Turkey
Turkmenistan
Uganda
Ukraine
United Arab Emirates
United Kingdom
United States
Uruguay
Uzbekistan
Vanuatu
Venezuela
Vietnam
Western Samoa
Yemen
Yugoslavia
Zambia
Zimbabwe

APPENDIX E. *Variables list*

Concept	Description	Obs	Mean	SD	Min	Max	Source
DEPENDENT VARIABLES							
Independent Regulator	Independent regulator: year establishing a separate regulator; 1 = yes, 0 = no	5,656	.176	.381	0	1	ITU-Reg, various years
Privatization	Privatization: first privatization efforts; 1 = yes, 0 = no	5,434	.124	.329	0	1	ITU-Reg, various years
INDEPENDENT VARIABLES							
International Organization							
GATT-WTO member	Membership in the GATT and/or WTO in a given year	5,657	.600	.489	0	1	WTO website: www.wto.int
OECD member	Membership in the OECD in a given year	6,254	.162	.368	0	1	OECD Website; www.oecd.org
CONTROLS							
International markets							
Trade openness	Exports + Imports/GDP; natural log,	4,610	73.43	45.95	1.12	439.	(WDI) various years
Capital openness	Capital account openness on a scale of 0–9 (closed to most open), which counts how many of the nine openness criteria a country meets.	4,384	2.01	2.81	0	9	IMF *Annual Report on Exchange Arrangements and Exchange Restrictions* (AREAR) (Brune, Guisinger, and Garrett 2002)

APPENDIX E. (*cont.*)

Concept	Description	Obs	Mean	SD	Min	Max	Source
Domestic							
Teledensity (fixed)	Mainlines per 1,000 people; natural log	4,594	3.50	1.88	−2.3	6.62	ITU
Country Size	Population; natural log,	6,096	15.38	1.93	10.1	20.9	(WDI) various years
Level of Development	GDP per capita, in 1995 U.S. constant dollars (log)	4,895	7.52	1.52	4.33	10.9	(WDI)

Unit = country-year. All explanatory variables are lagged one period. GATT, General Agreement on Tariffs and Trade; GDP, gross domestic product; ITU, International Telecommunications Union; OECD, Organization for Economic Cooperation and Development; WTO, World Trade Organization

APPENDIX F. *Results: Weibull hazard ratios for telecom reform*

	Independent Regulator	Privatization
International Organizations		
GATT-WTO member	2.69***	1.88**
	(.72)	(.60)
OECD member	1.83**	1.90*
	(.58)	(.73)
Controls:		
International markets		
Trade (IM+EX/GDP)	.99	1.00
	(.00)	(.00)
Capital Openness (0–9 closed to open)	1.04	1.00
	(.00)	(.04)
Domestic		
Teledensity (fixed)	1.15	1.18
	(.13)	(.17)
Income		
(ln GDP per capita	.83	1.04
	(.13)	(.19)
Diffusion		
Global reforms: prior regulators (or privatizations)	1.00	.99
	(.72)	(.28)
Observations	2652	2848
Number of subjects	166	164
Number of failures	116	86

Results reported as hazard ratios. Standard errors reported in parentheses. *** = significant at the .001 level; ** = significant at the .05 level, * = significant at the .10 level. GATT, General Agreement on Tariffs and Trade; GDP, gross domestic product; OECD, Organization for Economic Cooperation and Development; WTO, World Trade Organization

APPENDIX G. *The dependent variable: Regulatory reform in telecommunications in Central and Eastern Europe*

	Czech Republic	Hungary	Poland	Slovakia
Population (mil.)	10.5 (2009)	10.0 (2009)	38.1 (2009)	5.4 (2009)
GDPpc ppp	$18,200 (2009)	$12,900 (2009)	$11,200 (2009)	$16,200 (2009)
Liberalization	Yes	Yes	Yes	Yes
Local	2001			
Long distance	2001			
International	2001			
Privatization of Incumbent Telecom Operator	Yes – partial then full	Yes – full	Yes – partial	Yes – partial
	1994: SPT Telecom jsc (Správa post a telekomunikaci) 1995: Privatization (partial) of Czech Telecom (CT) 2003: Deprivatization, CT bought out shares	1992: Matáv converted into joint stock co. 1993: Matáv full privatization to strategic investors	1992: Joint stock co. of TPSA, Telekomunikacja Polska Spolka Akcyjna	1994: Joint stock company formed, Slovak Telecom 2000: Slovak Telecom privatized; 51% shares sold to Deutsche Telekom
Separate Regulator	1992: Separate regulator in Ministry of Economy	1989: Office created in Ministry	1990: Separate regulatory office in Ministry	1993: Separate regulatory office established; Slovak Telecom Office

	1996: In Ministry of Transport and Communications 2000: Czech Telecom Office est. as independent regulator 2004: Further steps 2005: Authorized as market regulator	1993: Communications Authority of Hungary (Hif) established; separate regulator 2000: Independent regulator established; 2003: Further steps under NRF	2001: Independent regulator, TPSA established 2003–4: Further steps under NRF	2000: STO becomes independent regulator 2002: STO moves into own building; 2004: More under NRF
Regulator Network	Independent Regulators Group (00) European Regulators Group (04) BEREC	Independent Regulators Group (00) European Regulators Group (04) BEREC	Independent Regulators Group (00) European Regulators Group (04) BEREC	Independent Regulators Group (00) European Regulators Group (04) BEREC
Competition in Fixed?	Yes	Yes	No	No
Competition in Mobile? (# of firms)	Yes (3)	Yes (3)	Yes (3)	Yes (2)

APPENDIX H. *The dependent variable: Regulatory reform in telecommunications in Northern Europe*

	Denmark	Finland	Netherlands	Sweden
Population	5.3 million	5.1 million	15.8 million	8.9 million
GDPpc ppp (2002 est.)	$39,661	$32,284	$31,287	$33,665
Separate Regulator	Telestyrelsen – National IT and Telecom Agency (NITA)	Viestintävirasto Kommunikationsverket (FICORA)	Onafhankelijke Post en Telecommunicatie Autoriteit (OPTA) 1997	Post and Telestyrelsen (PTS)
Privatization of Incumbent Telecom Operator	Yes	No	Yes	–
	TeleDanmark: Partially privatized in 1994; fully privatized now	Telecom Finland remains state owned	KPN is partially state owned	Telia
Regulator Network	Independent Regulators Group (00) European Regulators Group (04) BEREC	Independent Regulators Group (00) European Regulators Group (04) BEREC	Independent Regulators Group (00) European Regulators Group (04) BEREC	Independent Regulators Group (00) European Regulators Group (04) BEREC
Competition in Fixed?	Yes	Yes	Yes	Yes
Competition in Mobile? (# of firms)	Yes	Yes	Yes	Yes

APPENDIX I. *European Regulatory Authorities (2011)*

Austria	Rundfunk und Telekom Regulierungs-GmbH	RTR
Belgium	Institut Belge des services Postaux et de Télécommunications	BIPT
Bulgaria	Communications Regulation Commission	CRC
Croatia	Hrvatska agencija za poštu i elektroničke komunikacije	HAKOM
Cyprus	Office of the Commissioner of Telecommunications and Postal Regulation	OCTPR
Czech Republic	Český telekomunikační úřad	CTU
Denmark	Telestyrelsen – National IT and Telecom Agency	NITA
Estonia	Konkurentsiamet	ECA
Finland	Viestintävirasto Kommunikationsverket	FICORA
France	Autorité de Régulation des Communications électroniques et des Poste	ARCEP
Germany	Bundesnetzagentur	BNetzA
Greece	National Telecommunications and Post Commission	EETT
Hungary	Nemzeti Media Hírközlési Hatóság	NMHH
Iceland	Póst- og fjarskiptastofnun	PTA
Ireland	Commission for Communications Regulation	ComReg
Italy	Autorità per le garanzie nelle comunicazioni	AGCom
Latvia	Sabiedrisko pakalpojumu regulesanas komisija	SPRK
Liechtenstein	Amt für Kommunikation	AK
Lithuania	Rysiu reguliavimo tarnybos	RRT
Luxembourg	Institut Luxembourgeois de Régulation	ILR
Macedonia, former Yugoslav Republic of	Agency for Electronic Communications of the Republic of Macedonia	AEC
Malta	Malta Communications Authority	MCA
Netherlands	Onafhankelijke Post en Telecommunicatie Autoriteit	OPTA

APPENDIX I. (*cont.*)

Norway	Post og teletilsynet	PT
Poland	Urząd Komunikacji Elektronicznej	UKE
Portugal	Autoridade Nacional de Comunicações	ANACOM
Romania	Autoritatea Naţională pentru Administrare şi Reglementare în Comunicaţii	ANCOM
Slovak Republic	Telekomunikacný úrad Slovenskej republiky	TO SR
Slovenia	Agencija za pošto in elektronske komunikacije Republike Slovenije	APEK
Spain	Comisión del Mercado de las Telecomunicaciones	CMT
Sweden	Post & Telestyrelsen	PTS
Switzerland	Commission fédérale de la communication/Office fédéral de la communication	COMCOM
Turkey	Bilgi Teknolojileri ve İletişim Kurumu	TK
United Kingdom	Office of Communications	OFCOM

APPENDIX J. *Abbreviations and Acronyms*

ADC	Access deficit charges
ADSL	Asymmetric digital subscriber line
APEC	Asia-Pacific Economic Cooperation forum
BDT	Telecommunications Development Bureau of the ITU
BEREC	Body of European Regulators of Electronic Communication
BOC	Bell Operating Company
CATV	Cable television
CITEL	Inter-American Telecommunications Commission
CLEC	Competitive local exchange carrier
CPP	Calling party pays
DNS	Domain Name System
DSL	Digital subscriber line
DSU	Dispute Settlement Understanding
EC	European Commission
ECJ	European Court of Justice
ECTEL	East Caribbean Regulatory Telecommunications Authority
EU	European Union
FCC	Federal Communications Commission
GATS	General Agreement on Trade in Services
GBT	Group on Basic Telecommunications (WTO)
GSM	Global system for mobile communication
HDSL	High bit-rate digital subscriber line
ICT	Information and communication technologies
ILEC	Incumbent local exchange carrier
IP	Internet protocol
ISDN	Integrated services digital network
ISO	International Satellite Organization
ISO	International Standards Organization
ISP	International Settlements Policy
ISP	Internet service provider
IT	Information technology
ITU	International Telecommunications Union
ITU-T	International Telecommunication Standardization Sector
IXP	Internet exchange point
JV	Joint venture
LECs	Local exchange carriers
LRAIC	Long-run average incremental costs
LRIC	Long-run incremental costs
MFN	Most favored nation

APPENDIX J. (*cont.*)

NP	Number portability
NRA	National regulatory authority
NSP	Net settlements payments
OECD	Organization for Economic Cooperation and Development
OECS	Organization of Eastern Caribbean States
PC	Personal computer
PCI	Price cap index
PCS	Personal communication service
POI	Point of interconnection
PSTN	Public switched telephone network
PTO	Public telecommunications operator
PTT	Post, Telegraph and Telephone Administration
PUC	Public Utility Commission
QoS	Quality of service
RBHC	Regional Bell Holding Company
RBOC	Regional Bell Operating Company
RIO	Reference interconnection offer
ROR	Rate of return
RPP	Receiving party pays
SADC	Southern Africa Development Community
SATCC	Southern Africa Transport and Communications Commission
SMP	Significant market power
TCP/IP	Transmission control protocol/Internet protocol
TRASA	Telecommunications Regulators Association of Southern Africa
TELRIC	Total element long run incremental cost
TSLRIC	Total service long run incremental costs
UMTS	Universal mobile telecommunications system
UN	United Nations
US$	United States dollars
USO	Universal service obligation
VANS	Value-added network services
VAS	Value-added services
VSAT	Very small aperture terminal
WLL	Wireless local loop
WTO	World Trade Organization
WTSA	World Telecommunications Standardization Assembly

References

Acharya, Amitav. 2004. How Ideas Spread: Whose Norms Matter? Norm Localization and Institutional Change in Asian Regionalism. *International Organization* 58 (2): 239–75.

Allison, Paul David. 1984. *Event History Analysis: Regression for Longitudinal Event Data*. Beverly Hills, CA: Sage Publications.

Anderson, Robert. 1999. "Slovakia Seeks to Reassure Foreign Investors." London: *Financial Times*, September 13, p.3.

—2004. "Cesky Telecom Set for Offering State Sell-Off." London: *Financial Times*, November 16, p. 31.

—2005. "Telefonica Bid for 51% Cesky Stake in Balance." London: *Financial Times*, April 1, p. 26.

Appel, Hilary. 2004. *A New Capitalist Order: Privatization and Ideology in Russia and Eastern Europe*. Pittsburgh, PA: University of Pittsburgh Press.

Avant, Deborah D., Martha Finnemore, and Susan K. Sell (eds.). 2010. *Who Governs the Globe?* New York: Cambridge University Press.

BEREC, Body of European Regulators of Electronic Communication. berec.europa.eu. Accessed August 25, 2012.

Bar, Francois, and Michael Borrus. 1992. Information Networks and Competitive Advantage: Issues for Government Policy and Corporate Strategy. *International Journal of Telecommunications Management* 7 (6/7/8): 398–408.

Barnes, Andrew. 2003. Comparative Theft: Context and Choice in the Hungarian, Czech, and Russian Transformations, 1989–2000. *East European Politics and Societies* 17 (3): 533–65.

Barnett, Michael, and Martha Finnemore. 2004. *Rules for the World: International Organizations in Global Politics*. Ithaca, NY: Cornell University Press.

Bartlett, David L. 1997. *The Political Economy of Dual Transformations: Market Reform and Democratization in Hungary*. Ann Arbor, MI: University of Michigan Press.

Bates, Robert, and Anne O. Krueger, eds. 1993. *Political and Economic Interactions in Economic Policy Reform*. Cambridge, MA: Blackwell.

Beck, Thorsten, George Clarke, Alberto Groff, Philip Keefer, and Patrick Walsh. 2001. New Tools in Comparative Political Economy: The Database of Political Institutions. *World Bank Economic Review 15* (1): 165–76.

Bennett, Colin J. 1991. What Is Policy Convergence and What Causes It? *British Journal of Political Science 21*: 215–33.

Berger, Suzanne, and Ronald Dore, (eds.). 1996. *National Diversity and Global Capitalism*. Ithaca, NY: Cornell University Press.

Berry, Frances Stokes, and William D. Berry. 1992. Tax Innovation in the American States: Capitalizing on Political Opportunity. *American Journal of Political Science 36* (3): 714–42.

Biersteker, Thomas J. 1995. The "Triumph" of Liberal Economic Ideas in the Developing World. In *Global Change, Regional Response: The New International Context of Development*, ed. Barbara Stallings (pp. 174–98). New York: Cambridge University Press.

Blanchard, Olivier, Rudiger Dornbusch, Paul Krugman, Richard Layard, and Lawrence Summers. 1991. *Reform in Eastern Europe*. Cambridge, MA: MIT Press.

Blossfeld, Hans-Peter, and Götz Rohwer. 2002. *Techniques of Event History Modeling: New Approaches to Causal Analysis*, 2nd ed. Mahwah, NJ: Lawrence Erlbaum Associates.

Blyth, Mark. 1997. Any More Bright Ideas? The Ideational Turn of Comparative Political Economy. *Comparative Politics* 29: 229–50.

Bobinski, Christopher. 1996. "Polish Telecom Monopoly Set to Stay Until Sell-off Starts." London: *Financial Times*, December 24, p.3.

—1999. "Polish Telecommunications Industry Up for Grabs." London: *Financial Times*, August 23, p. 24.

Boix, Carles. 1998. *Political Parties, Growth and Equality. Conservative and Social Democratic Economic Strategies in the World Economy*. New York: Cambridge University Press.

Boland, Vincent. 1995. "Western Europe Telecoms Look East – Saturation Prompts Search for New Markets." London: *Financial Times*, July 4, p. 24.

Box-Steffensmeier, Janet M., and Bradford S. Jones. 2004. *Event History Modeling: A Guide for Social Scientists*. New York: Cambridge University Press.

Boylaud, Olivier, and Giuseppe Nicoletti. 2000. "Regulation, market structure and performance in telecommunication." *Economic Department Working Papers No. 237 ECO/WKP(2000)10*. Paris: OECD.

Brady, Henry E., and David Collier, (eds.) 2004. *Rethinking Social Inquiry: Diverse Tools, Shared Standards*. New York: Rowman & Littlefield Publishers Inc.

Brinks, Daniel, and Michael Coppedge. 2006. Diffusion Is No Illusion: Neighbor Emulation in the Third Wave of Democracy. *Comparative Political Studies* 39 (4): 463–89.

Brooks, Sarah Marie. 2009. *Social Protection and the Market in Latin America: The Transformation of Social Security Institutons*. New York: Cambridge University Press.

Brown, Ashley C., Jon Stern, Bernard Tenenbaum; with Defne Gencer. 2006. *Handbook for Evaluating Infrastructure Regulatory Systems*. Washington, DC: World Bank.

Bruce, Robert R., Ioannis Nicolaos Kessides, and Lothar Kneifel. 1999. *Overcoming Obstacles to Liberalization of the Telecom Sector in Estonia, Poland, the Czech Republic, Slovenia, and Hungary: An Overview of Key Policy Concerns and Potential Initiatives to Facilitate the Transition Process*. Washington, DC: World Bank.

Brune, Nancy, Alexandra Guisinger, and Geoffrey Garrett. 2002. "*The Political Economy of Capital Account Liberalization*." Working Paper. New Haven, CT: Yale University.

Bútorovà, Zora, and Martin Bútora. 1995. Political Parties, Value Orientations and Slovakia's Road to Independence. *In Party Formation in East-Central Europe*, ed. Gordon Wightman (pp. 107–133). Aldershot, UK: Edward Elgar.

Cameron, James, and Karen Campbell. 1998. *Dispute Resolution in the WTO*. London: Cameron May.

Campbell, John L., and Ove K. Pedersen. 2007. Institutional Competitiveness in the Global Economy: Denmark, the United States, and the Varieties of Capitalism. *Regulation and Governance* 1 (3): 230–46.

Castells, Manuel. 2007. *Mobile Communication and Society: A Global Perspective: A Project of the Annenberg Research Network on International Communication*. Cambridge, MA: MIT Press.

Cave, Martin, and Leonard Waverman. 1998. The Future of International Settlements. *Telecommunications Policy* 22 (11): 883–98.

Central Intelligence Agency (CIA). 2005–2011. World Factbooks. https://www.cia.gov/library/publications/the-world-factbook/. Accessed on August 25, 2010.

Cerny, Philip. 1995. Globalization and the Changing Logic of Collective Action. *International Organization* 49 (4): 595–625.

Checkel, Jeffrey T. 2005. International Institutions and Socialization in Europe: Introduction and Framework. *International Organization* 59 (4): 801–26.

Coase, Ronald H. 1960. The Problem of Social Cost. *The Journal of Law and Economics* 3: 1–44.

Coen, David, and Adrienne Heritier. 2005. *Redefining Regulatory Regimes: Utilities in Europe*. Cheltenham, UK: Edward Elgar.

Cogburn, Derrick L. 2003. Governing Global Information and Communications Policy: Emergent Regime Formation and the Impact on Africa. *Telecommunications Policy* 27, 135–53.

Commission of the European Communities. 2003a. *Comprehensive Monitoring Report on Hungary's Preparation for Membership*. Brussels: European Union.

—2003b. *Comprehensive Monitoring Report on Poland's Preparations for Membership*. Brussels: European Union.

—2003c. *Comprehensive Monitoring Report on Slovakia's Preparations for Membership*. Brussels: European Union.

—2003d. *Comprehensive Monitoring Report on the Czech Republic's Preparations for Membership*. Brussels: European Union.

Cowhey, Peter F. 1990. The International Telecommunications Regime: The Political Roots of Regimes for High Technology. *International Organization* 44 (2): 169–99.

Cowhey, Peter F., Jonathan David Aronson, and Donald Abelson. 2009. *Transforming Global Information and Communication Markets: The Political Economy of Innovation*. Cambridge, MA: MIT Press.

Cowhey, Peter F., and Mikhail M. Klimenko. 2001. *The WTO Agreement and Telecommunication Policy Reforms*. Washington, DC: World Bank Development Research Group Trade.

Cox, Gary W., and Mathew D. McCubbins. 2001. The Institutional Determinants of Economic Policy Outcomes. In *Presidents, Parliaments, and Policy*, eds. Stephan Haggard and Mathew D. McCubbins (pp. 21–63). New York: Cambridge University Press.

CTO, Czech Telecommunications Office. 2003. *Report on the Activities of the Czech Telecommunications Office for 2002*. Prague, Czech Republic: Czech Telecommunications Office.

Cudahy, Richard D. 1998. The Folklore of Deregulation (with Apologies to Thurman Arnold). *Yale Journal on Regulation* 15 (2): 427–42.

D'Souza, Juliet, and William L. Megginson. 1999. The Financial and Operating Performance of Privatized Firms During the 1990s. *Journal of Finance* 54 (4): 1397–1438.

Danish Ministry of Research (Forskningsministeriet). 1995. *Bedst og billigst gennem reel konkurrence*. Copenhagen: Danish Ministry of Research.

Danish National IT and Telecom Agency (NITA). 2010. Copenhagen: NITA.

de Bijl, Paul, and Martin Peitz. 2000. *Competition and Regulation in the Netherlands*. The Hague: CPB Netherlands Bureau for Economic Policy Analysis.

Denton, Nicholas. 1993. "Survey of International Telecommunications." London: *Financial Times*, October 18, p. XIV.

—1994. "Survey of the Czech Republic." London: *Financial Times*, November 4, p. 21.

Deutsch, Karl W. 1966. *The Nerves of Government*. New York: The Free Press.

Done, Kevin. 1997. "Survey – Slovakia; Government Is Stalling Over Sell-Off." London: *Financial Times*, March 25, p. 2.

—1998. "E Europe Lines Up to Sell Telecoms." London: *Financial Times*, January 9, p. 2.

Dornisch, David. 2001. Competitive Dynamics in Polish Telecommunications, 1990–2000: Growth, Regulation, and Privatization of an Infrastructural Multi-Network. *Telecommunications Policy 25* (6): 381–407.

Drezner, Daniel W. 2005. Globalization, Harmonization, and Competition: The Different Pathways to Policy Convergence. *Journal of European Public Policy* 12 (5): 841–59.

—2007. *All Politics Is Global: Explaining International Regulatory Regimes*. Princeton, NJ: Princeton University Press.

EIU, Economist Intelligence Unit. 1999–2010. *Country Profiles for Czech Republic, Denmark, Finland, Hungary, the Netherlands, Poland, Slovakia and Sweden*. London: The Economist. http://www.eiu.com/Default.aspx. Accessed September 10, 2012.

Elkins, Zachary, Tom Ginsburg, and James Melton. 2009. *The Endurance of National Constitutions*. New York: Cambridge University Press.

Epstein, Rachel A. 2008. *In Pursuit of Liberalism: International Institutions in Postcommunist Europe*. Baltimore, MD: Johns Hopkins University Press.

European Bank for Reconstruction and Development (EBRD). 1995. *EBRD Telecommunications Regulatory Status Survey*. London: EBRD.

European Commission. 2009. Final Report 2009. *15th Progress Report on the Single European Electronic Communications Market – 2009*. Report and Country Charts. http://ec.europa.eu/information_society/

policy/ecomm/doc/implementation_enforcement/annualreports/15threport/comm_en.pdf. Last modified August 25, 2010.

—2010a. Digital Agenda: Broadband Speeds Increasing but Europe Must Do More. Report and Country Charts. *Digital Agenda for Europe, 2010*. http://ec.europa.eu/information_society/newsroom/cf/item-detail-dae.cfm?item_id=6502&language=default. Accessed September 10, 2012.

—2010b. Digital Agenda Scoreboard." *Digital Agenda for Europe, 2010*. http://ec.europa.eu/information_society/digital-agenda/scoreboard/index_en.htm. Accessed September 10, 2012.

FCC, Federal Communications Commission. 2004. "IMTS Accounting Rates of the United States, 1985–2003." http://www.fcc.gov/ib/pd/pf/account.html#sec3. Accessed June 2004.

FICORA, Finnish Communications Regulatory Authority. 2010–12. *Telecommunications Markets in the Nordic Countries*. Helskinki: FICORA. http://www.ficora.fi/en/index/tutkimukset/generalmarketinformation.html. Accessed on August 25, 2012.

Fink, Carsten, Aaditya Mattoo, and Randeep Rathindran. 2003. An Assessment of Telecommunications Reform in Developing Countries. *Information Economics & Policy 15*: 443–66.

Finnemore, Martha. 1993. International Organizations as Teachers of Norms. *International Organization* 47 (4): 565–97.

—1996. *National Interests in International Society*. Ithaca, NY: Cornell University Press.

Fisher, Richard W. 2000. Trade in Telecommunications Services. In *Speech by Ambassador Richard W. Fisher, Deputy United States Trade Representative, delivered to the House Commerce Subcommittee on Telecommunications, Trade and Consumer Protection*. Washington, DC.

Frieden, Jeffry A., and Ronald Rogowski. 1996. The Impact of the International Economy on National Policies: An Analytical Overview. In *Internationalization and Domestic Politics*, eds. Robert O. Keohane and Helen V. Milner (pp. 25–47). Cambridge, UK: Cambridge University Press.

Frydman, Roman, and Andrzej Rapaczynski. 1994. *Privatization in Eastern Europe: Is the State Withering Away?* Budapest: Central European University.

Garrett, Geoffrey. 1998. *Partisan Politics in the Global Economy*. New York: Cambridge University Press.

Gilardi, Fabrizio. 2005. The Institutional Foundations of Regulatory Capitalism: The Diffusion of Independent Regulatory Agencies in Western Europe. *Annals of the American Academy of Political and Social Science 598*: 84–101.

—2008. *Delegation in the Regulatory State: Independent Regulatory Agencies in Western Europe*. Cheltenham; Northampton, MA: Edward Elgar.

Goldman, Minton F. 1998. *Slovakia Since Independence*. Westport, CT: Praeger.

Gourevitch, Peter. 1986. *Politics in Hard Times: Comparative Responses to International Economic Crises*. Ithaca, NY: Cornell University Press.

Grabbe, Heather. 2006. *The EU's Transformative Power: Europeanization Through Conditionality in Central and Eastern Europe*. London: Palgrave Macmillan.

Gray, Virginia. 1973. Innovation in the States: A Diffusion Study. *American Political Science Review* 67 (4): 1174–85.

Grunberg, Isabelle. 1998. Double Jeopardy, Globalization, Liberalization, and the Fiscal Squeeze. *World Development* 26 (4): 591–605.

Grzymała-Busse, Anna. 2002. *Redeeming the Communist Past: The Regeneration of Communist Parties in East Central Europe*. New York: Cambridge University Press.

Gutierrez, Luis H., and Sanford Berg. 2000. Telecommunications Liberalization and Regulatory Governance: Lessons from Latin America. *Telecommunications Policy* 24 (10/11): 865–84.

Haas, Ernst B. 1964. *Beyond the Nation-State. Functionalism and International Organization*. Palo Alto, CA: Stanford University Press.

Haas, Peter M. 1992. Introduction: Epistemic Communities and International Policy Coordination. *International Organization* 46 (1): 1–35.

Hahn, Robert W. 2000. *Reviving Regulatory Reform: A Global Perspective*. Washington, DC: AEI-Brookings Joint Center for Regulatory Studies.

Hall, Peter A. 1993. Policy Paradigms, Social Learning, and the State: The Case of Economic Policymaking in Britain. *Comparative Politics* 25 (3): 275–96.

Hall, Peter A., and David Soskice, (eds.). 2001. *Varieties of Capitalism: The Institutional Foundations of Comparative Advantage*. New York: Oxford University Press.

Hanley, Eric, Lawrence King, and István Tóth János. 2002. The State, International Agencies, and Property Transformation in Post-Communist Hungary. *American Journal of Sociology 108* (1): 129–67.

Hašek, Jaroslav. 1930. *The Good Soldier Schweik*. Trans. Paul Selver. New York: Doubleday, Doran and Company.

Heller, Krisztina. 1994. Restructuring in Hungary. In *Implementing Reforms in the Telecommunications Sector*, eds. Bjorn Wellenius and Peter A. Stern (pp. 375–382). Washington, DC: World Bank.

Henisz, Witold J. 2000. The Institutional Environment for Economic Growth. *Economics and Politics* 12 (1): 1–31.

Henisz, Witold J., and Bennet A. Zelner. 2001. The Institutional Environment for Telecommunications Investment. *Journal of Economics and Management Strategy* 10: 123–47.

Henisz, Witold J., Bennet A. Zelner, and Mauro F. Guillen. 2005. The Worldwide Diffusion of Market-Oriented Infrastructure Reform, 1977–1999. *American Sociological Review* 70 (6): 871–98.

Henten, Anders. 2004. Telecoms in Denmark: Investment, Performance, and Regulation. In *WDR (World Dialogue on Regulation for Network Economies) Dialogue Theme 2003*, pp. 1–36. http://www.regulateonline.org/content/view/206/65/. Accessed on August 25, 2012.

Henten, Anders, and Thomas Wulff. 1996. Danish Telecommunications: Keeping the Policy Options Open. *Telecommunications Policy* 20 (9): 669–84.

Héritier, Adrienne, Christoph Knill, and Susanne Mingers. 1996. *Ringing the Changes in Europe: Regulatory Competition and the Transformation of the State: Britain, France, Germany*. In De Gruyter Studies in Organization series. Berlin; New York: W. de Gruyter.

Hosmer, David W., Jr., and Stanley Lemeshow. 1999. *Applied Survival Analysis: Regression Modeling of Time to Event Data*. New York: John Wiley & Sons, Inc.

Hrubý, Zdenek. 1997. Czech Republic: Towards Limited Competition and Streamlining Regulation. In *Telecommunications Take-Off in Transition Countries*, eds. Karl-Ernst Schenk, Jürn Kruse, and Jürgen Müller (pp. 139–66). Brookfield, VT: Ashgate Publishing Company.

International Center for Economic Growth, European Center. 2003. The expected effects of EU accession on the telecommunication sector of the Visegrad countries. http://icegec.com/events/docs/iceg_amcham/telecom_summary.pdf. Accessed February 3, 2004.

International Telecommunications Union (ITU). 2002. *Competition Policy in Telecommunications: The Case of Denmark*. Geneva, Switzerland: International Telecommunications Union.

—2010. *World Telecommunications Indicators Database 1960–2010*. International Telecommunications Union. Geneva, Switzerland. http://www.itu.int/ITU-D/ict/publications/world/world.html

—2011a. Trends in Telecommunications Reform, 1999–2010. http://www.itu.int/ITU-D/treg/publications/trends12.html

—2011b. *Yearbook of Statistics: Chronological Time Series 2001–2010*. Geneva, Switzerland. http://www.itu.int/ITU-D/ict/publications/yb/index.html

—2011c. *The World in 2009–2011. ICT in Facts and Figures*. Geneva, Switzerland. http://www.itu.int/ITU-D/ict/facts/2011/index.html

Intven, Hank, Jeremy Oliver, and Edgardo Sepulveda, for McCarthy Tétrault. 2000. *Telecommunications Regulation Handbook*. Washington, DC: World Bank.

Jacobsen, John Kurt. 1995. Much Ado About Ideas: The Cognitive Factor in Economic Policy. *World Politics* 47: 283–310.

Jacoby, Wade. 2004. *The Enlargement of the EU and NATO: Ordering from the Menu in Central Europe*. New York: Cambridge University Press.

—2008. Minority Traditions and Postcommunist Politics: How Do IGOs Matter? In *Transnational Actors in Central and East European Transitions*, eds. Mitchell A. Orenstein, Stephen Bloom, and Nicole Lindstrom (pp. 56–76). Pittsburgh, PA: University of Pittsburgh Press.

Johnson, Juliet. 2006. Two-Track Diffusion and Central Bank Embeddedness: The Politics of Euro Adoption in Hungary and the Czech Republic. *Review of International Political Economy* 13 (3): 362–86.

Johnson, Simon, and James Kwak. 2011. *13 Bankers: The Wall Street Takeover and the Next Financial Meltdown*. New York: Vintage Books.

Johnston, Alastair Iain. 2008. *Social States: China in International Institutions 1980–2000*. Princeton, NJ: Princeton University Press.

Jordana, Jacint, and David Levi-Faur. 2006. Towards a Latin American Regulatory State? The Diffusion of Autonomous Regulatory Agencies Across Countries and Sectors. *International Journal of Public Administration* 29 (4–6): 335–66.

Kahn, Alfred E. 2001. *Whom the Gods Would Destroy, Or How Not to Deregulate*. Washington, DC: AEI-Brooks Joint Center for Regulatory Studies.

Katzenstein, Peter K. 1985. *Small States in World Markets: Industrial Policy in Europe*. Ithaca, NY: Cornell University Press.

Kelley, Judith. 2004. *Ethnic Politics in Europe: The Power of Norms and Incentives*. Princeton, NJ: Princeton University Press.

Keohane, Robert O., and Helen Milner. 1996. *Internationalization and Domestic Politics*. New York: Cambridge University Press.

Keohane, Robert O., and Joseph S. Nye. 1977. *Power and Interdependence: World Politics in Transition*. Boston, MA: Little, Brown & Company.

Kopstein, Jeff, and David Reilly. 2000. Geographic Diffusion and the Transformation of the Postcommunist World. *World Politics* 53 (1): 1–37.

Krasner, Stephen D. 1991. Global Communications and National Power: Life on the Pareto Frontier. *World Politics* 43 (3): 336–66.

Krueger, Anne O. 1974. The Political Economy of the Rent-Seeking Society. *American Economic Review* 83 (June): 291–303.

Krueger, Anne O., and Chonira Aturupane. 1998. *The WTO as an International Organization*. Chicago: University of Chicago Press.

La Porta, Rafael, Florencio Lopez-de-Silanes, Andrei Shleifer, and Robert W. Vishny. 1997. Legal Determinants of External Finance. *Journal of Finance* 52 (3): 1131–50.

Laffont, Jean-Jacques, and Jean Tirole. 2000. *Competition in Telecommunications*. Cambridge, MA: MIT Press.

Lazer, David. 2001. Regulatory Interdependence and International Governance. *Journal of European Public Policy* 8 (3): 474–92.

Lazer, David, and Viktor Mayer-Schönberger. 2002. Governing Networks: Telecommunication Deregulation in Europe and the United States. *Brooklyn Journal of International Law* 27 (3): 819–51.

Lee, Chang Kil, and David Strang. 2006. The International Diffusion of Public-Sector Downsizing: Network Emulation and Theory-Driven Learning. *International Organization* 60 (Fall): 883–909.

Levi-Faur, David. 1999. Governing Dutch Telecommunications Reform: State-Business Interactions in the Transformation of National Policy Regimes to (European) Embedded Policy Regimes. *Journal of European Public Policy* 6 (1): 101–22.

—2005. The Global Diffusion of Regulatory Capitalism. In *Annals of the American Academy of Political and Social Science*, eds. David Levi-Faur and Jacint Jordana. Vol. 598: 12–32. Thousand Oaks, CA: Sage Publications, Inc.

Levi-Faur, David, and Jacint Jordana, eds. 2005. The Rise of Regulatory Capitalism: The Global Diffusion of a New Order, Vol. 598. *The Annals of the American Academy of Political and Social Science*. Thousand Oaks, CA: Sage Publications, Inc.

Levy, Brian, and Pablo T. Spiller. 1994. The Institutional Foundations of Regulatory Commitment: A Comparative Analysis of Telecommunications Regulation. *Journal of Law, Economics and Organization* 10 (2): 201–46.

—(eds.). 1996. *Regulations, Institutions, and Commitment. Comparative Studies of Telecommunications*. Cambridge: Cambridge University Press.

Li, Wei, and Lixin Colin Xu. 2002. The Political Economy of Privatization and Competition: Cross-Country Evidence from the Telecommunications Sector. *Journal of Comparative Economics* 30 (3): 439–62.

Madden, G., and S. Savage. 1998. CEE Telecommunications Investment and Economic Growth. *Information Economics & Policy* 10: 173–95.

Maggetti, Martino. 2009. The role of Independent Regulatory Agencies in Policy-Making: A Comparative Analysis. *Journal of European Public Policy* 16 (3): 450–70.

Majone, Giandomenico. 1996. *Regulating Europe.* New York: Routledge.

—2000. The Credibility Crisis of Community Regulation. *Journal of Common Market Studies (Wiley Blackwell) 38* (2): 273–302, 306.

Mansell, R., A. Davies, and W. Hulsink. 1996. The New Telecommunications in the Netherlands: Strategy, Policy and Regulation. *Telecommunications Policy* 20 (4): 273–89.

Marsden, Christopher T. 2011. *Internet Co-Regulation: European Law, Regulatory Governance and Legitimacy in Cyberspace.* Cambridge, UK; New York: Cambridge University Press.

Marsh, Peter. 1995. "EBRD Annual Meeting: Telecom Rivalry Vital to Growth." London: *Financial Times*, April 29, p. 4.

Martin, Lisa L., and Beth A. Simmons. 1998. Theories and Empirical Studies of International Institutions. *International Organization* 52 (4): 729–57.

McDermott, Gerald A. 2002. *Embedded Politics: Industrial Networks and Institutional Change in Postcommunism.* Ann Arbor, MI: University of Michigan Press.

McNamara, Kathleen R. 1998. *The Currency of Ideas: Monetary Politics in the European Union.* Ithaca, NY: Cornell University Press.

Megginson, William L., and Jeffrey M. Netter. 2001. From State to Market: A Survey of Empirical Studies on Privatization. *Journal of Economic Perspectives* 39 (2): 321–89.

Melody, William H. 2002. *Trends in European Telecommunication: 2002 Status Report of Denmark's Progress in Telecom Reform and Information Infrastructure Development.* Lyngby: LIRNE.

Mintrom, Michael. 1997. Policy Entrepreneurs and the Diffusion of Innovation. *American Journal of Political Science* 41 (3): 738–70.

Mosley, Layna. 2003. *Global Capital and National Governments.* New York: Cambridge University Press.

MTI-Econews. 1990. "Government Discusses Property Policy Guidelines for 1991." http://www.mtieco.hu/Pages/Login.aspx?lang=eng. Accessed September 9, 2010.

—1991. "Proposal on Privatization Strategies in Hungary." http://www.mtieco.hu/Pages/Login.aspx?lang=eng. Accessed September 9, 2010.

Mueller, Milton. 2010. *Networks and States: The Global Politics of Internet Governance.* Cambridge, MA: MIT Press.

Murillo, Maria Victoria. 2001. *Labor Unions, Partisan Coalitions and Market Reforms in Latin America*. New York: Cambridge University Press.

Murrell, Peter. 1993. What Is Shock Therapy? What Did It Do in Poland and Russia? *Post-Soviet Affairs* 9 (2): 111–40.

Newbery, David M. 1991. Reform in Hungary: Sequencing and Privatization. *European Economic Review* 35 (2–3): 571–80.

Nicoletti, Giuseppe, and Frederic Pryor. 2001. *Subjective and Objective Measures of the Extent of Governmental Regulations*. Paris: OECD.

Noam, Eli M. 1998. *Telecommunications in Latin America*. New York: Oxford University Press.

Noll, Roger G., and Frances McCall Rosenbluth. 1995. Telecommunications Policy: Structure, Process, Outcomes. In *Structure and Policy in Japan and the United States*, eds. Peter F. Cowhey and Mathew D. McCubbins. New York: Cambridge University Press.

North, Douglass C. 1990. *Institutions, Institutional Change and Economic Performance*. New York: Cambridge University Press.

Nulty, Timothy E. 1994. Challenges and Issues in Central and Eastern European Telecommunications. In *Implementing Reforms in the Telecommunications Sector: Lessons from Experience*, eds. Björn Wellenius and Peter A. Stern (pp. 339–52). Washington, DC: The International Bank for Reconstruction and Development/World Bank.

Nye, Joseph S., Jr. 2002. *The Paradox of American Power: Why the World's Only Superpower Can't Go It Alone*. New York: Oxford University Press.

O'Dwyer, Conor. 2006. *Runaway State-Building: Patronage Politics and Democratic Development*. Baltimore, MD: Johns Hopkins University Press.

OECD. 1997. *The OECD Report on Regulatory Reform: Synthesis*. Paris: OECD.

—1999. *OECD Reviews of Regulatory Reform: Regulatory Reform in the Netherlands 1999*. Paris: OECD Publishing. doi: 10.1787/9789264173774-en.

—2000a. *OECD Reviews of Regulatory Reform: Regulatory Reform in Denmark 2000*. Paris: OECD Publishing. doi: 10.1787/9789264189386-en

—2000b. *OECD Reviews of Regulatory Reform: Regulatory Reform in Hungary 2000*. Paris: OECD Publishing. doi: 10.1787/9789264181908-en

—2000c. Telecommunications Regulations: Institutional Structures and Responsibilities. In *DSTI/ICCP/TISP(99)15/FINAL*. Paris: OECD.

—2001. *OECD Reviews of Regulatory Reform: Regulatory Reform in the Czech Republic 2001*. Paris: OECD Publishing. doi: 10.1787/9789264194816-en

—2002a. *OECD Reviews of Regulatory Reform: Poland 2002: From Transition to New Regulatory Challenges*. Paris: OECD Publishing. doi: 10.1787/9789264176034-en

—2002b. *Regulatory Policies in OECD Countries: From Interventionism to Regulatory Governance*. Paris: OECD Publishing. doi: 10.1787/9789264177437-en.

—2003. *OECD Reviews of Regulatory Reform: Finland 2003: A New Consensus for Change*. Paris: OECD Publishing. doi: 10.1787/9789264102699-en

—2007. *OECD Reviews of Regulatory Reform: Sweden 2007: Achieving Results for Sustained Growth*. Paris: OECD Publishing. doi: 10.1787/9789264009103-en

—2011. *Communications Outlook 1999–2011 (published biennially)*. Paris: OECD. http://www.oecd.org/sti/broadbandandtelecom/oecdcommunicationsoutlook2011.htm. Accessed September 12, 2012.

Orenstein, Mitchell A. 2001. *Out of the Red: Building Capitalism and Democracy in Postcommunist Europe*. Ann Arbor: University of Michigan Press.

—2008. *Privatizing Pensions: The Transnational Campaign for Social Security Reform*. Princeton, NJ: Princeton University Press.

Padgett, Stephen. 2003. Between Synthesis and Emulation: The Processes and Outcomes of EU Policy Transfer in the Policy Sector. *Journal of European Public Policy* 10: 227–46.

Page, Arthur W. 1941. *The Bell Telephone System*. New York: Harper & Brothers Publishers.

Pelkmans, Jacques, and Andrea Renda. 2011. *Single eComms Market? No Such Thing*. Centre for European Policy Studies. www.ceps.eu/ceps/download/4201

Peltzman, Sam. 1976. Toward a More General Theory of Regulation. *Journal of Law and Economics* 19 (2): 211–40.

Petrazzini, Ben A. 1995. *The Political Economy of Telecommunications Reform in Developing Countries. Privatization and Liberalization in Comparative Perspective*. Westport, CT: Praeger.

Pigou, Arthur C. 1938. *The Economics of Welfare*, 4th edition. London: Macmillan.

Polanyi, Karl. 1957. *The Great Transformation*. Boston: Beacon Press.

Pool, Ithiel de Sola, and Eli M. Noam. 1990. *Technologies Without Boundaries: On Telecommunications in A Global Age*. Cambridge, MA: Harvard University Press.

Ramamurti, Ravi. 1996. *Privatizing Monopolies: Lessons from the Telecommunications and Transport Sectors in Latin America.* Baltimore, MD: The Johns Hopkins University Press.

Raustiala, Kal. 2002. The Architecture of International Cooperation: Transgovernmental Networks and the Future of International Law. *Virginia Journal of International Law* 43. http://papers.ssrn.com/sol3/papers.cfm?abstract_id=333381

Reed, John. 2000. "Poland – Better Late Than Never for TPSA." London: *Financial Times*, April 27, p. 30.

Reinhart, Eric. 2001. Adjudication Without Enforcement in GATT Disputes. *Journal of Conflict Resolution* 45 (2): 174–95.

Risse-Kappen, Thomas. 1994. Ideas Do Not Float Freely: Transnational Coalitions, Domestic Structures, and the End of the Cold War. *International Organization* 48: 185–214.

Risse, Thomas. 2000. Let's Argue! Communicative Action in World Politics. *International Organization* 54 (1): 1–39.

Robinson, Anthony. 1995. "Survey of International Telecommunications." London: *Financial Times.*

Rogers, Everett M. 1995. *Diffusion of Innovations*, 4th ed. New York: Free Press.

Roland, Gerard. 2000. *Transition and Economics: Politics, Markets, and Firms.* Cambridge, MA: MIT Press.

Röller, Lars-Hendrick, and Leonard Waverman. 2001. Telecommunications Infrastructure and Economic Development: A Simultaneous Approach. *American Economic Review* 91 (4): 909–23.

Rudra, Nita. 2002. Globalization and the Decline of the Welfare State in Less-Developed Countries. *International Organization* 56 (2): 411–45.

Sachs, Jeffrey D. 1993. *Poland's Jump to the Market Economy.* Cambridge, MA: MIT Press.

Sallai, Gyula, Ivan Schmideg, and George Lajtha. 1996. Telecommunications in Central and Eastern Europe: Similarities, Peculiarities and Trends of Change in the Countries of Transition. *Telecommunications Policy* 21 (5): 325–40.

Sandholtz, Wayne. 1993. Institutions and Collective Action: The New Telecommunications in Western Europe. *World Politics* 45 (2): 242–70.

Schamis, Hector. 2002. *Re-forming the State: The Politics of Privatization in Latin America and Europe.* Ann Arbor: University of Michigan Press.

Schimmelfennig, Frank, Stefan Engert, and Heiko Knobel. 2003. Costs, Commitment and Compliance: The Impact of EU Democratic Conditionality on Latvia, Slovakia and Turkey. *Journal of Common Market Studies* 41 (3): 495–518.

Schimmelfennig, Frank, and Ulrich Sedelmeier. 2005. *The Politics of European Union Enlargement: Theoretical Approaches*. New York: Routledge.

Schmidt, Vivien A. 2002. Europeanization and the Mechanics of Economic Policy Adjustment. *Journal of European Public Policy* 9 (6): 894–912.

Schwartz, Andrew H. 2006. *The Politics of Greed: How Privatization Structured Politics in Central and Eastern Europe (World Social Change)*. New York: Rowman & Littlefield.

Sell, Susan. 1998. *Power and Ideas: North-South Politics of Intellectual Property and Antitrust*. Albany, NY: State University of New York (SUNY) Press.

Sharkey, William W. 1982. *The Theory of Natural Monopoly*. New York: Cambridge University Press.

Shelanski, Howard A. 2002. From Sector-Specific Regulation to Antitrust Law for US Telecommunications: The Prospects for Transition. *Telecommunications Policy* 26: 335–55.

Simmons, Beth A., Frank Dobbin, and Geoffrey Garrett. 2006. Introduction: The International Diffusion of Liberalism. *International Organization* 60: 781–810.

—eds. 2008. *The Global Diffusion of Markets and Democracy*. New York: Cambridge University Press.

Singer, J. D., and Willett, J. B. 1993. It's About Time: Using Discrete-Time Survival Analysis to Study Duration and the Timing of Events. *Journal of Educational Statistics*, *18*, 155–95.

Singh, J. P. 2008. *Negotiation and the Global Information Economy*. Cambridge; New York: Cambridge University Press.

—1999. *Leapfrogging Development: The Political Economy of Telecommunications Restructuring*. Albany, NY: State University of New York (SUNY) Press.

—2002. "Negotiating Regime Change: The Weak, the Strong, and the WTO Telecom Accord." In *Information Technologies and Global Politics: The Changing Scope of Power and Governance*, ed. James N. Rosenau, and J. P. Singh (pp. 239–74). Albany, NY: State University of New York (SUNY) Press.

Slaughter, Anne-Marie. 2004. *A New World Order*. Princeton, NJ: Princeton University Press.

Stark, David, and Laszlo Bruszt. 1998. *Post-Socialist Pathways: Transforming Politics and Property in Eastern Europe*. New York: Cambridge University Press.

Steiner, Faye. 2000. Regulation, Industry Structure and Performance in the Electricity Supply Industry. In *Economics Department Working Papers No. 238 ECO/WKP(2000)11*. Paris: OECD.

Stern, Jon. 1994. Economic Regulation in Central and Eastern Europe. *Economics of Transition* (September): 391–7.

Stigler, George. 1971. The Theory of Economic Regulation. *Bell Journal of Economics and Management Service* 2: 3–21.

Stiglitz, Joseph E. 2002. *Globalization and Its Discontents*. New York: Norton.

—2010. *Freefall: America, Free Markets, and the Sinking of the World Economy*. New York: W. W. Norton & Co.

Stone, Randall W. 2002. *Lending Credibility: The International Monetary Fund and the Post-Communist Transition*. Princeton, NJ: Princeton University Press.

Strang, David. 1991. Adding Social Structure to Diffusion Models: An Event History Framework. *Sociological Methods Research 19* (3): 324–53.

Strang, David, and Sarah A. Soule. 1998. Diffusion in Organizations and Social Movements: From Hybrid Corn to Poison Pills. *Annual Review of Sociology* 24: 265–90.

Strange, Susan. 1996. *The Retreat of the State: The Diffusion of Power in the World Economy*. New York: Cambridge University Press.

Teichman, Judith. 2001. *The Politics of Freeing Markets in Latin America*. Chapel Hill, NC: University of North Carolina Press.

Thatcher, Mark. 1999. *The Politics of Telecommunications: National Institutions, Convergence, and Change in Britain and France*. New York: Oxford University Press.

—2002. Regulation After Delegation: Independent Regulatory Agencies in Europe. *Journal of European Public Policy* 9 (6): 954–72.

—2007. Regulatory Agencies, the State and Markets: A Franco-British Comparison. *Journal of European Public Policy* 14 (7): 1028–47.

Vachudova, Milada Anna. 2005. *Europe Undivided: Democracy, Leverage, & Integration After Communism*. New York: Oxford University Press.

Vickers, John, and George K. Yarrow. 1988. Privatization: An Economic Analysis. In *MIT Press Series on the Regulation of Economic Activity, Vol. 18*. Cambridge, MA: MIT Press.

Viscusi, W. Kip, John M. Vernon, and Joseph E. Harrington. 2000. *Economics of Regulation and AntiTrust*, 3rd ed. Cambridge, MA: MIT Press.

Vogel, Steve. 2006. Why Freer Markets Need More Rules. In *Creating Competitive Markets: The Politics and Economics of Regulatory Reform*, eds. Martin A. Levin, Marc K. Landy, and Martin Shapiro (pp. 25–42). Washington, DC: Brookings Institution Press.

Vogel, Steven K. 1996. *Freer Markets, More Rules: Regulatory Reform in Advanced Industrial Countries*. Ithaca, NY: Cornell University Press.

Vreeland, James Raymond. 2003. *The IMF and Economic Development.* New York: Cambridge University Press.
Wagstyl, Stefan. 2001. "Survey: Investing in Central and Eastern Europe." London: *Financial Times*, July 2, p. 2.
Walker, Jack L. 1969. The Diffusion of Innovations Among the American States. *The American Political Science Review 63* (3): 880–99.
Wallsten, Scott J. 2001. An Econometric Analysis of Telecom Competition, Privatization and Regulation in Africa and Latin America. *Journal of Industrial Economics* 49 (1): 1–19.
—2001. Telecom Traffic and Investment in Developing Countries: The Effects of International Settlement Rate Reductions. *Journal of Regulatory Economics 20* (3): 307–23.
—2002. Does Sequencing Matter? Regulation and Privatization in Telecommunications Firms. *World Bank Working Paper*. Washington, DC: World Bank.
Waverman, Leonard, and Pantelis Koutroumpis. 2011. Benchmarking Telecoms Regulation: The Telecommunications Regulatory Governance Index (TRGI). *Telecommunications Policy 35* (5): 450–68.
Welfens, Paul J. 1995. Telecommunications and Transition in Central and Eastern Europe. *Telecommunications Policy 19* (7): 561–77.
Wellenius, Björn. 1989. *Restructuring and Managing the Telecommunications Sector. A World Bank Symposium*. Washington, DC: World Bank.
—1993. Telecommunications: World Bank Experience and Strategy. *World Bank Discussion Papers 192*. Washington, DC: World Bank.
Wellenius, Björn, and Gregory C. Staple. 1996. *Beyond Privatization: The Second Wave of Telecommunications Reforms in Mexico.* Washington, DC: World Bank.
Wellenius, Björn, and Peter A. Stern. 1994. *Implementing Reforms in the Telecommunications Sector: Lessons from Experience*. Washington, DC: World Bank.
Weyland, Kurt. 2006. *Bounded Rationality and Policy Diffusion: Social Sector Reform in Latin America*. Princeton, NJ: Princeton University Press.
Wibbels, Erik. 2005. *Federalism and the Market: Conflict and Economic Reform in the Developing World*. New York: Cambridge University Press.
Wilson, Bruce. 2007. Compliance by WTO Members with Adverse WTO Dispute Settlement Rulings: The Record to Date. *Journal of International Economic Law 10* (2): 397–403.
Wilson, Ernest J., and Kelvin R. Wong. 2007. Negotiating the Net in Africa: The Politics of Internet Diffusion. In *Ipolitics*. Boulder, CO: Lynne Rienner.

World Bank. 1975–2010. *World Development Indicators*. Washington, DC: World Bank. http://data.worldbank.org/data-catalog/world-development-indicators. Accessed on August 25, 2012.

World Trade Organization (WTO). 1995–2010. *Telecommunications Services*. http://www.wto.org/english/tratop_e/serv_e/telecom_e/telecom_e.htm. Accessed on August 25, 2012.

Xavier, Patrick. 2000. Market Liberalisation and Regulation in Hungary's Telecommunications Sector. *Telecommunications Policy* 24 (10/11): 807–41.

Yamaguchi, Kazuo. 1991. *Event History Analysis*. Newbury Park, CA: Sage.

Yee, Albert S. 1996. The Causal Effects of Ideas on Policies. *International Organization* 50 (1): 69–108.

Zacher, Mark W., and Brent A. Sutton. 1996. *Governing Global Networks: International Regimes for Transportation and Communications*. New York: Cambridge University Press.

Ziegler, J. Nicholas. 1997. *Governing Ideas: Strategies for Innovation in France and Germany* Ithaca, NY: Cornell University Press.

Index